D1616644

METHOD FOR THE ONE-KEYED FLUTE

Method for the One-Keyed Flute

Baroque and Classical

Janice Dockendorff Boland

University of California Press

BERKELEY • LOS ANGELES • LONDON

UNIVERSITY OF CALIFORNIA PRESS
Berkeley and Los Angeles, California

University of California Press, Ltd.
London, England

Library of Congress Cataloging-in-Publication Data

Boland, Janice Dockendorff.
    Method for the one-keyed flute / Janice
Dockendorff Boland.
        p.   cm.
    Includes bibliographical references.
    ISBN 0-520-21447-1 (paper : alk. paper)
    1. Flute—Methods.   I. Title.
MT342.B765   1998
788.3'2193—dc21   97-49641
                                                        CIP
                                                        MN

Printed in the United States of America

9 8 7 6 5 4 3 2 1

The paper used in this publication meets the minimum
requirements of American National Standard for Information
Sciences—Permanence of Paper for Printed Library Materials,
ANSI Z39.48-1984.

To Elcy,
who supports me in all that I do.
With gratitude and love.

CONTENTS

PREFACE

Musicians today are caught up in a movement to study and explore the use of old musical instruments. The flute generating the most interest is the eighteenth-century one-keyed flute. A growing number of flutists are purchasing modern replicas and learning to play them.

Not long ago the one-keyed flute was considered an inadequate predecessor of the modern flute. In 1966 René LeRoy (p. 14) described the eighteenth-century flute as a "very imperfect instrument." The writer of a doctoral essay at Eastman said that the one-keyed flute's inferior pitch quality and inferior tone quality were natural and unavoidable flaws in the instrument (Hartman, 1961, p. 16). Generally, flutists had no desire to learn to play this simple one-keyed instrument when a "perfected" flute was available to them.

However, attitudes have changed during the past thirty to forty years. Concerts and professional recordings featuring historic flutes are no longer rarities. Workshops specializing in the manufacture of historical flutes and music publishers specializing in scholarly editions of early music support these performance activities.

Flutists who experiment with the one-keyed flute find that it is indeed an instrument of merit. Innate in the simplicity of its structure are unique expressive qualities not inherent in the modern Boehm-system flute.

This method book is written for players of the Boehm-system flute who are already familiar with tone production and modern flute technique: it is designed to help with the flutist's initial approach to the one-keyed flute. The *Method* can serve as a self-guiding tutor or as a text when the flutist is working with a teacher. It is not intended to be a musicological treatise, but a practical and useful guide which cites historical sources. These historical sources offer a broad diversity of opinions which challenge us to explore the ideas of eighteenth-century writers and incorporate them into our present-day experience.

The *Method* addresses such topics as choosing a flute and assembling the instrument, to more advanced concepts such as tone color and eighteenth-century articulation patterns. Discussions of tone, intonation, and tonality will help guide the student in exploring the expressive nature of the instrument. Fingering charts, exercises, and eighteenth-century tunes will help the student get started. To encourage the reader to explore primary historical sources, the "Top 13" eighteenth-century flute tutors are reviewed with reference given to present-day facsimile editions and translations. Those new to the one-keyed flute will be helped by the annotated repertoire list of easy solos, duets, and studies. The annotated bibliography references both historical and modern sources.

Many texts on eighteenth-century technique and style are currently available, both as primary sources (from eighteenth-century authors) and secondary sources (in this case, twentieth-century writings regarding eighteenth-century performance style). The scope of this book does not allow for any more than a mention of some of the more important techniques and performance styles. Textbooks and articles by leading scholars are referenced throughout the text and included in the annotated bibliography to encourage the reader to become familiar with these important sources.

Your reasons for exploring the one-keyed flute may range from mere curiosity to a desire to master the instrument for the purposes of public performance. Even if you wish only to experiment with the one-keyed flute, doing so will give you important insights that you will find useful for modern, Boehm-system flute performances.

EDITORIAL CONVENTIONS

To avoid extensive footnotes, publication date (and page numbers where there are quotations) of the sources referenced are given in parentheses within the text following the author's name. Complete bibliographic entries are found in the annotated bibliography.

In quoting foreign language sources, references are made to available English translations. For example, page numbers for quotes of the Quantz tutor refer to the Reilly translation listed in the bibliography.

The exercises and tunes in Chapter Four come from eighteenth- and nineteenth-century flute tutors and collections. The exercises or tunes credit the composer (where known), the author (in the case of a treatise which has not identified the composer of its tunes), or the title of a collection. Edited slurs are shown by means of a dashed slur. Breath mark indications are mine, with the exception of the little duet in e minor by Blavet, who frequently indicated his own breaths. Trills very often begin from the note above the principal note—there are exceptions. The performance suggestions for the tunes in this *Method* are based on the instruction given in the tutor from which the tune was taken.

I have used the letters d'–b' for notes of the first octave, c"–b" for the second octave, and c'"–a'" for the third octave.

I have used the capital letter when describing a particular major key, such as G major, and a lower case letter when describing a minor key, such as e minor.

To simplify the layout, fingerings in Chapter Four are given using a simple number system instead of the graphics found on the charts. For example, g' is designated 1 2 3 / _ _ _ .

ACKNOWLEDGMENTS

My deepest gratitude

To Amy Boland, Joyce Bryant, Betsy Colvin, Betsy Cuffel, Andrew Cox, David Dahl, John Dowdall, Christopher Krueger, Betty Bang Mather, Roger Mather, Judy Moore, Ardal Powell, Jama Stilwell, Teresa Texeira, John Thow, and Richard M. Wilson for advice offered after reading the text, in full or in part. To Richard M. Wilson and Christopher Krueger for guidance in writing the chapter on intonation. I take responsibility for all the errors and omissions which remain.

To flute-maker Friedrich von Huene for permission to reprint his excellent drawings of original instruments.

To Stephen Preston for information, insights, and inspiration given at annual baroque flute master classes at the Wildacres Flute Symposium since 1985.

To Barbara Kallaur for repertoire ideas.

To Betty Rogers, Linda Bloedel, Harlene Hansen, and Richard Doyle at Stewart Memorial Library at Coe College for assistance with interlibrary loan materials. To The University of Iowa Libraries for making their materials available. To David Lasocki at Indiana University for answering many reference questions.

To the Iowa Arts Council and the National Endowment for the Arts for a Creative Artist's Grant to assist in readying the book for the publisher.

To McGinnis & Marx Music Publishers for permission to reprint my survey of eighteenth-century tutors from *Fluting and Dancing: Articles and Reminiscences for Betty Bang Mather on her 65th Birthday* (New York: McGinnis & Marx, 1992).

To John Dowdall and Elsie Kleese, my ardent supporters in whatever I strive to do.

And most of all, to Betty Bang Mather, my mentor and friend, who has given me a wealth of instruction, advice, and encouragement. Her pioneering work with the one-keyed flute, her patient, masterful teaching, her exemplary musicianship, and her many contributions to the scholarly world have been my inspiration.

Marion, Iowa   J.D.B.
December 1997

CHAPTER I

ABOUT THE ONE-KEYED FLUTE

Illustration from Johann Phillip Eisel, *Musicus autodidaktos.*
Erfurt: Johann Michael Funcken, 1738

ON THE FLUTE

The one-keyed flute was developed from the keyless, cylindrical-bored Renaissance flute, possibly by 1660. Its beginnings are sketchy at best. Historians have traditionally credited the Hotteterre and Philidor families at the French court of Louis XIV with the "perfection" of the flute. New evidence has challenged that position (Powell, 1996), but we, as yet, have nothing to replace it. Regardless, early one-keyed flutes had three sections: a more-or-less cylindrical head joint, a conical middle joint with six tone holes, and a foot joint with one tone hole covered by a key. Later, probably by about 1720, makers divided the middle section into two parts.

A Bit of History

The one-keyed flute, with some modification, was in use for well over one hundred years. Many professional flutists used it as the instrument of preference to near the end of the eighteenth-century. Some amateurs used the one-keyed flute even longer. One could purchase a one-keyed wooden flute in the Sears, Roebuck Catalogue in the United States in 1908 for $1.55.

In the eighteenth century, the flute was the most popular of all wind instruments. It was considered very fashionable, as evidenced by Frederick the Great of Prussia's great passion for the instrument. Composers found a market for flute music among both amateurs and professionals, and consequently the eighteenth century is rich in flute literature.

Names

The one-keyed flute has many names. Eighteenth-century tutors refer to it as the one-keyed flute, the cross or transverse flute (*la flûte traversière, die Querflöte,* or *flauto traverso*), and the German flute (*flûte d'Allemagne*). (Be aware that in the early part of the eighteenth century, the simple term "flute" [*flauto*] usually referred to the recorder.) Today the instrument is variably referred to as the "one-keyed flute," the "baroque flute" (certainly appropriate for the early eighteenth-century instrument), or the "traverso," a shortened version of its Italian name. I shall refer to it as the one-keyed flute.

Materials Used

Historically, one-keyed flutes have been made mostly of wood. Quantz (1752) declared boxwood to be the most common and durable, but he preferred ebony for its clear and beautiful tone. Tromlitz (1791) said both ebony and grenadilla produced a flute tone that was brighter and stronger than boxwood. Kingwood and ivory were also used. However, ivory was used more often to decorate wooden flutes, and many flutes featured ivory ferrules at each joint and an ivory end cap.

The range of the one-keyed flute is d' to a'''. However, I recommend that the beginner limit the first efforts to the more traditional range of d' to e'''.

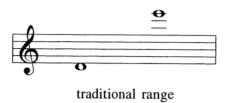

traditional range

During the first part of the eighteenth century, the highest practical note was considered to be e'''. Hotteterre (1707, pp. 45-46) writes:

> The notes above e''' are forced notes, and cannot enter naturally in any piece. Furthermore you must not persist in wanting to find them at the beginning, as it is a trouble which you must spare yourself until you are very advanced.

Quantz (1752, p. 57) agrees, saying, "The highest usable note that you can invariably produce is e'''. Those which are higher require a particularly good embouchure."

The third octave f is a bad note on some instruments. Hotteterre (1707, p. 46) finds that it "can almost never be done on the flute" and omitted it from his fingering chart. The third octave f sharp and g are easier to play.

Despite the difficulties of the third octave, it is not uncommon to find the flute's range extended beyond e'''. One notable example is J. S. Bach's *Partita in a minor* for solo flute where we find an a''' at the end of the first movement.

In the latter part of the eighteenth century, notes beyond e''' appear with increasing frequency. Flute construction during this period tended to favor the high register a little more and the third octave spoke with greater ease.

ON THE PARTS OF THE FLUTE

Because there were many instrument makers, and because the one-keyed flute evolved and changed over the course of more than a century, many variations of the one-keyed flute exist. Although some makers added keys, foot registers, and tuning slides, the simpler one-keyed flute described below was the most standard flute in use during the eighteenth century and remained in use well past the beginning of the nineteenth century.

The earliest one-keyed flute had three parts: a head joint, a middle joint, and a foot joint. Today one such three-piece flute is referred to as the "Hotteterre" flute because it resembles one with distinctive ornamental turnings attributed to the Hotteterre family of instrument makers.

Three-Piece Flute

A "Hotteterre" Flute

By about 1720, makers had divided the middle joint of the flute into two parts, an upper-middle joint and a lower-middle joint. Four-piece flutes are replicated more frequently by today's flute makers than the three-piece instrument described above.

Four-Piece Flute

head joint...........upper-middle joint...lower-middle joint...foot joint

The tenon is that part of the flute joint which fits into the socket of the adjacent joint. Tenons are traditionally wrapped in thread (silk, cotton, or linen) that has been rubbed with wax.[1] Modern replicas sometimes have cork-covered tenons. Regardless of whether the tenons are wrapped with cork or thread, they must be waxed or greased regularly.

The Tenon

---

[1] See Tromlitz, *Unterricht* (1791), transl. Powell, 33–37 to learn how to wrap the tenons with thread.

The cork at the end of the head joint is movable and its placement is critical for good intonation. First, set the cork somewhere between .75 and 1 inch (20–25 millimeters) from the center of the blow hole. An easy way to measure cork placement is with a wooden dowel rod. Purchase a 12-inch (30 centimeters) length measuring about one-half inch (12.5 millimeters) in diameter (available at craft shops or lumber yards) and simply measure and mark the dowel rod with a pencil about .75 inch (20 millimeters) from one end. The dowel rod, placed inside the head joint, serves the same purpose as the metal rod furnished with today's modern flutes; adjust the head cork so that the pencil mark falls in the center of the embouchure hole.

Next, you must further refine the cork's placement to suit your own way of playing. Each flutist may have a slightly different cork placement, reflecting individual embouchures and ways of blowing. Using the fingerings from the Basic Fingering Chart on page 63, tune d' with d" and d'". If the octaves are true, the cork placement is correct. However, if you find the d's are not in tune, you will need to adjust the cork (and subsequently your pencil mark on the dowel rod). Quantz (1752, p. 33) recommends the following adjustments.

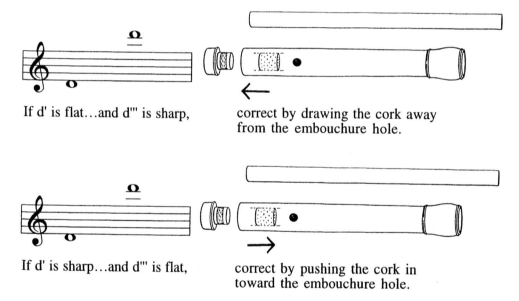

If d' is flat...and d'" is sharp,   correct by drawing the cork away from the embouchure hole.

If d' is sharp...and d'" is flat,   correct by pushing the cork in toward the embouchure hole.

The cork must also be adjusted if the player chooses to use a longer or shorter upper-middle joint. (See *Corps de réchange* on page 9.) Lengthening or shortening the flute in this way disturbs the correct proportions of the instrument and the intonation suffers.[2] To remedy this problem, the cork is pushed in toward the embouchure hole when a long upper joint is used and drawn back when a short upper joint is used. The cork can be moved by using the same half-inch dowel rod you used to measure the cork placement.

[2] See Tromlitz, *Unterricht* (1791), transl. Powell, 33 for a discussion of why the flute is thrown out of tune when exchanging the upper middle joints.

Some flutes are fashioned with a screw attached to the cork. The screw cap is a simple mechanism for adjusting the position of the cork and is especially useful when changing middle joints. The player simply turns the end cap to draw the cork out. The following illustration of a Quantz head joint (Reilly translation of Quantz, *Versuch,* 1985) shows the cork with a screw attached.

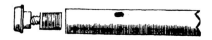

The Screw Cap

Some flutes may have a foot register, which is a telescoping, adjustable foot joint useful for making adjustments in tuning when changing middle joints. The foot joint is made a little shorter for each shorter middle piece (*corps de réchange*). Some makers of modern replicas offer the foot register as an option. Quantz (1752) was among those eighteenth-century flutists who strongly opposed the use of the foot register because, in his opinion, it throws the flute out of tune.

Flute with a Foot Register

ON PITCH

Pitch was not standardized in the eighteenth century. It varied greatly from country to country, from city to city, and even within the same city. We find evidence that flutists were required to play at every imaginable pitch standard from very low (A-c.392 and lower) to very high (A-440 and higher).

Quantz's (1752) personal preference was for lower-pitched flutes, which he found to be more pleasing, moving, and majestic; he found higher-pitched instruments to be more penetrating.

A-415 has been adopted as a useful compromise for today's performers of most baroque music. Modern replicas of one-keyed flutes are most commonly, but not exclusively, made at A-415.

Modern Replicas

Modern replicas may also be pitched a whole step low (A-c.392) or lower. "French chamber pitch," as this is sometimes called, is appropriate for the music of early eighteenth-century French composers and the music of J. S. Bach, and was the preference of Frederick the Great.

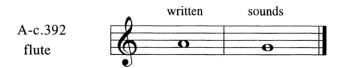

Some twentieth-century flute makers will make a modern replica at A-440, referred to as "modern pitch," to accommodate players who are working with other musicians using this pitch standard.

The one-keyed flute is used today in several professional orchestras which specialize in the use of period instruments. Baroque orchestras usually require the use of flutes tuned at A-415. However, Classical orchestras have established a higher pitch as a basis for tuning and require a one-keyed flute (or more keys for later Classical repertoire) tuned at A-430 or even higher.

Corps de réchange

It would of course have been impractical for eighteenth-century flutists to own many instruments, each built to a different pitch. The more practical solution to the need for flexibility to play at varying pitch standards was in place by about 1720. According to Quantz (1752) flute makers began to make anywhere from two to six or more upper-middle joints of varying lengths.[3] The French call these interchangeable joints *corps de réchange*.

The use of longer *corps de réchange* lowers the pitch, and the use of shorter *corps de réchange* raises the pitch, allowing the flutist to play at different pitch standards.

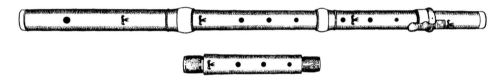

Flute with two *corps de réchange*

Some makers of modern replicas make a flute with two or more *corps de réchange*. For instance, one may be tuned at A-415 and one at A-392. This way the flutist can own one instrument, yet has the ability to play at two pitch standards. An adjustment of the cork is necessary when changing joints. When playing at A-415 the player uses the shorter *corps de réchange* and draws the cork away from the embouchure hole.

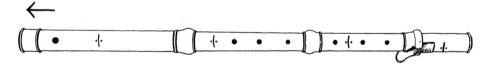

Move the cork away from the embouchure hole
when playing at A-415

[3] Traverso-player Christopher Krueger told me that most surviving eighteenth-century flutes with *corps de réchange* show significant wear on only one *corp*, and the playing characteristics vary considerably with each one. Personal communication, October, 1997. Also see Tromlitz, *Unterricht* (1791), transl. Powell, 33–37 for more information about *corps de réchange*.

When playing at A-392, the player uses the longer *corps de réchange* and pushes the cork in toward the blow hole.

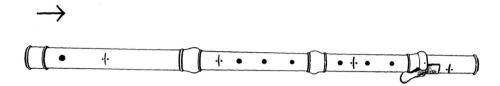

Draw the cork in toward the embouchure hole
when playing at A-392

Be aware that it is very difficult to design a one-keyed flute with two or more *corps de réchange* (and therefore two or more pitches) that plays equally well "in tune" at various lengths and pitches. Most often, one pitch has been favored, and the flute will simply play best in tune at that pitch. Discuss this concept with your flute maker to see how he or she has handled the problem.

ON CHOOSING A FLUTE

A good instrument that is tuned truly reduces the task of playing by half.

Quantz (1752, p. 51)

Today's players of one-keyed flutes can choose from among high-quality modern replicas made by craftsmen around the world, including the United States, Canada, Australia, Europe, South America, Russia, and Japan. Replicas are usually copies of specific historic flutes from the eighteenth century. And of course a few fine antique instruments are available on the market as well.

There are many decisions to be made when selecting a flute. Ask for assistance from a professional player. Also seek the guidance of flute makers who know by the orders they fill which flutes are most in demand. Look for a flute with good workmanship, with the tone color you desire, designed in a style to suit the music you will play, and that plays well in tune and is pitched according to your needs.

Three important decisions you will need to make are (1) the pitch of the flute, (2) the style of the flute, and (3) the type of wood used in its construction.

Determine what pitch you would like the flute to be. The common standard today for most baroque music is A-415. Choose a pitch that allows you to play with colleagues and friends. Does your harpsichordist normally tune the instrument to A-415? Is there another flutist with whom you wish to perform? What pitch is his or her flute? The tone of the flute is markedly different at different pitches. A higher-pitched flute is more brilliant and penetrating; a lower-pitched flute is softer and more mellow.

Pitch

You may wish to match the instrument to the music you will play or to the circumstances in which you will play. Will you do orchestral playing? Or will you find yourself more often in intimate chamber music settings? While some replicas can be used for a variety of music, others are more specialized or suited to a smaller range of styles. A flute designed for the music of Hotteterre won't be suitable for late eighteenth-century Mozart. Ask your flute maker for advice. Some popular reproductions today are modeled after instruments by Hotteterre (French maker, after Graz original c.1700), Denner (Nuremberg maker, after original played by Hünteler, early eighteenth century), Bressan (London maker, pre-1730), Rottenburgh (Brussels maker, after original in the

Style

11

Kuijken collection, c.1770), and August Grenser (Dresden maker, second half of the eighteenth century).

You may be asked what type of wood you prefer. Today's replicas are commonly made of boxwood, ebony, cocus wood, rosewood, or grenadilla. Grenadilla is the most dense and rosewood the least dense. The type of wood used in flute construction affects its tone quality, although modern makers tell me that the shape of the bore and cut of the tone and embouchure holes have a much more profound effect on the tone than the choice of wood. Try several and see which you prefer. A popular "beginning model" by Aulos of Japan is made of plastic. Because of international laws governing the sale of ivory, few replicas are made of ivory or have ivory trim. — Woods

Don't shy away from purchasing a used instrument. According to Quantz (1752, p. 51), "Generally a good and accurately tuned flute that has been frequently played is always preferable to a new one." — Used Flutes

ON CARE

Now if you have such a flute...spare no effort to maintain it so that it cannot be spoiled.

Tromlitz (1791, p. 40)

The one-keyed flute has its own unique set of requirements for proper care. Many fine flutes from the eighteenth century have survived, evidence that with proper care, a flute can last for centuries. I am indebted to flutemakers Roderick Cameron and Ardal Powell for much of the following information on flute care.

❑ Never store the flute in extreme heat or cold. Never allow your flute to lie exposed to the rays of the sun. Never leave the flute near a heating vent or fireplace. Never leave your flute in the trunk of your car in very cold or very hot weather. These cautionary measures will help guard against cracking.

❑ Never bring the flute into a warm room from the cold outdoors and play it immediately or it may crack. Don't blow warm air through the flute to warm it up. Allow it to gradually warm to room temperature.

❑ Never store the flute in low humidity environments. A wooden flute will dry out quickly in low humidity and may crack. Winter conditions in the Midwest and on the East coast of the United States produce low humidity factors, as do conditions in a heated home or studio. As a measure of prevention, carry a commercial humidifier (look in tobacco shops for a tiny humidifier the size of a tube of lipstick called a Humistat) in the case during the dry winter months; check it frequently and keep it damp. Store a wooden or ivory flute (in its box) in a plastic bag or plastic box (like a Tupperware container) during periods of low humidity and also when the flute is not in use for an extended period of time.

❑ Never assemble the flute if the joints feel too tight. If the tenons are wrapped with thread, adjust the wrappings for a proper fit.

❑ Never put the flute away wet in a horizontal position. Lindsay (1828–30) says that doing so will cause the water to accumulate on one side of the tube, expand that place, and throw the instrument out of tune for the moment; the flute will eventually rot from such treatment.

❑ Play a new flute or a newly acquired antique flute only ten minutes on the first day and gradually increase the playing time over a ten-day period. This allows the moisture on the player's breath to permeate the wood evenly, which helps to avoid cracking or warping the bore.

Checklist

13

- Lightly grease the tenons before each assembly. Use cork grease, petroleum jelly, or even Chapstick. Here is a recipe for homemade tenon grease: melt one part petroleum jelly (Vaseline) with one part beeswax, mix, and pour into a jar to cool.

- Swab the flute after each use to remove all moisture. A silk cloth is especially good for absorbing moisture; cotton is also good. Silk cloths on a long string, made for oboists, are available at music stores.

- If the flute is not swabbed or taken apart, place it upright on a peg so that the water may easily drain off.

- Wipe the outside surface with a soft, lint-free cloth.

- Be sure the tenons and sockets are dry before putting the flute away.

- If the pad on the key is sticky, apply a little talcum powder to the key pad.

- Keep the flute in a plastic bag when flying in the pressurized cabin of an aircraft. When the air pressure drops, the moisture is quickly sucked from a wooden flute.

- Oil a wooden flute regularly (about once a month) inside and out. A new flute will need to be oiled even more often until it is "played in."

Oiling the Flute

What type of oil should be used? The answer to this question depends in part on the flute you own. If you are playing an antique flute, it will be helpful to know that Quantz (1752) recommended almond oil. Tromlitz (1791) preferred rapeseed oil (also known today as canola oil), saying almond oil was too light and disappeared too quickly.

If you are playing a modern replica, contact the maker and ask what type of oil was used when the flute was crafted. It would be logical to use the same oil. Almond, canola, peanut, and olive oil are among the oils preferred today.

Linseed oil has been somewhat controversial, both in the eighteenth century and today. Lindsay (1828–30) recommended oiling the bore of the flute with cold-drawn linseed oil with a feather. However, Tromlitz (1791) found linseed oil to have too much substance and said it is known to form a crust inside the flute which changes the bore and spoils the flute. Flute maker Rod Cameron warns against the use of linseed oil, saying it is a hardening oil. Flute maker Ardal Powell reports that some makers of modern replicas use raw (not boiled) linseed oil as a finish because it forms a water repellent skin; these flutes can subsequently be oiled with raw linseed oil or other oils. I recommend avoiding the use of linseed oil unless it is recommended by your flute maker.

Before you begin to oil the flute, be sure the wood is dry—don't oil the flute immediately after you've played it. To protect the key pad from being damaged by oil, remove the key. Then be sure the key hole is free of oil before replacing the key. Or you may follow the advice of Lindsay (1828–30), who recommends placing a piece of paper, doubled, under the key pad before the oil is applied to keep the pad from absorbing the oil. Also consider removing the cork in the head joint before you begin oiling.

Now you are ready to oil the flute. First wrap an ordinary pipe cleaner around the end of a wooden chopstick to form a tight spiral about 1.25 inches (3 centimeters) long. Dip the stick into the oil and wipe it partially dry, then use it as a paintbrush in a spiral screw-thread motion down and through the bore of each joint. Tromlitz (1791) cautions us to use oil sparingly, saying that too much oil deprives the wood of its elasticity and damages the tone.

After letting the oil sit inside the bore of the flute for about half an hour, wipe out any excess with a paper towel rolled around a wooden chopstick.

Tromlitz (1791, p. 40) admonishes those who, believing that oil improves the tone, apply an excessive amount so that "it runs about inside" the flute.

CHAPTER II

LEARNING TO PLAY THE ONE-KEYED FLUTE

Illustration from Jacques Hotteterre, *Principes de la flûte traversière....*
Paris: Christophe Ballard, 1707.
Engraving by Bernard Picart. Perhaps a portrait of Jacques Hotteterre.

ON GETTING STARTED

He who wishes to excel in music must feel in himself a perpetual and untiring love for it, a willingness and eagerness to spare neither industry nor pains, and to bear steadfastly all the difficulties that present themselves in this mode of life.

Quantz (1752, p. 15)

You are embarking on a mission to learn a instrument totally different from the modern flute. The one-keyed flute is not inferior to the modern Boehm-system flute, as has been suggested by some twentieth-century writers; it is merely different. The flute in its one-keyed version suited the needs of music and musical expression for well over one hundred years. It is our challenge to explore that expressive capacity.

In this exploration, it is important to study the early flute tutors, for there is much to be learned. This text is full of references to the more important eighteenth-century tutors. However, we cannot simply mimic historical evidence, as ideas changed over the years and much of this historical information is conflicting. So in addition to studying historical references, the player will find it both necessary and rewarding to take cues from the flute itself and from its music, and to be influenced by the work done by players all over the world who have found a personal expression and brought this wooden flute to life in concerts and recordings.

How to Proceed

If you allow yourself time to learn the instrument before you expect too much, you won't be disappointed. Set aside a little time each day. In six months time you will be able to play pieces in the easier keys.

Assembly

Don't feel it necessary to arrange the embouchure hole and the tone holes in a straight line when you assemble the flute. Experiment to see what works best for you. Both Quantz (1752) and Devienne (c. 1792) tell us not to align the holes. Instead, they recommend that the head joint be turned inward so that the outer edge of the embouchure hole is in line with an imaginary line drawn down the center of the finger holes (see illustrations below by Tulou, 1853). This in effect allows the tone holes to be turned out, making it somewhat easier for the left hand to cover the open tone holes.

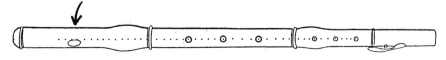

Rotate the head joint in slightly

If the flute is of the four-piece variety, you may align the tone holes, or you may choose to turn the lower-middle joint in toward your right hand. This position may benefit the hand position of the right hand. The foot joint should be rotated into a position that allows the little finger to easily reach the key.

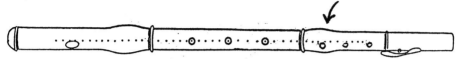

Rotate the lower-middle joint and the foot joint

ON HOLDING THE FLUTE

One must, by all means, observe not to make grimaces or to have ridiculous posture. The flute, being a noble instrument, is to be played in an agreeable manner.

Corrette (c. 1734, p. 26)

The modern Boehm-system flute and one-keyed flute differ in ways that affect how the one-keyed flute feels under the fingers. (1) First, the spacing of the tone holes is different. The tone holes of both the modern flute and the one-keyed flute are placed to allow for the best possible intonation. However, the one-keyed flute does not have sophisticated key work designed to accommodate the fingers as does the modern flute. The result is that the fingers must reach farther to cover some of the open holes. A beginning player is often frustrated while learning where the holes are under the fingers. (2) The thumb of the left hand has a different function. It must remain free on the modern flute to operate the b-keys. However, because there are no thumb-keys on the one-keyed flute, one may choose to hold the flute firmly with the thumb and first finger of the left hand, which forms a point of equilibrium. (3) The e-flat key is depressed for nearly all notes on the modern flute. Since it is depressed only occasionally on the one-keyed flute, the player's sense of balance in holding the instrument may be affected.

A word about care of the hands. Sadly, we all too frequently hear of musicians whose hands cease working properly for them—they encounter physical problems that create pain and dysfunction. You should know that some of these injured musicians report that the trouble started when they moved to a different or new instrument, therefore giving the muscular system something new to deal with. I broach this fearful subject as a way of cautioning you to begin the one-keyed flute, new to you and to your muscular system, slowly and with care. You will thank yourself later if you take the time in the first several weeks to develop a relaxed physical approach to finger placement.

Physical Problems

Since the tone holes of the one-keyed flute are farther apart than on modern flute, the fingers are required to achieve a broader stretch to cover the open holes. Avoid tensing the hands. Think instead of flopping the hand onto the flute and letting the fingers spread in a passive way to reach the holes. Try not to stretch the fingers laterally. Don't feel it necessary to hold

21

the fingers directly over their designated holes when the holes are not in use; allow the hand to relax when the fingers are resting above the flute. Most of all, don't do anything that results in pain.

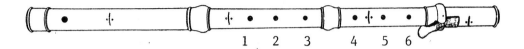

Lay the flute on the first (index) finger of the left hand so that it rests on the knuckle of the lowest joint. The index finger and the thumb support the flute. The first three fingers of the left hand cover tone holes 1, 2, and 3. The first and second fingers will be curved and the third a bit straighter. The little finger should not rest on the flute.

Left Hand

The right thumb is placed under the fourth tone hole or a little farther down the flute. The thumb should be set in the same place each time to ensure the proper position of the right fingers over their holes.

Right Hand

The first three fingers of the right hand cover tone holes 4, 5, and 6. Let the tips of the fingers of the right hand flop over the flute somewhat in a hand position you would consider incorrect on the modern flute; you will find that you can cover the holes more easily at a point closer to the first joint. One eighteenth-century flutist (Miller, c. 1799, p. 2) recommends covering the holes about an inch from the tip end of the finger, adding, "I never knew a Performer [to] have brilliant execution who covered the holes of the right hand with the tip ends of his fingers." An inch seems excessive to me, but experiment to see what is right for you.

Keep the little finger of the right hand relaxed and don't rest it on the flute when this finger is not in use. There is no need to keep the little finger extended in a ready-position to depress the key—such a position can only lead to physical problems. Some eighteenth-century flutists have dispensed bad advice regarding the placement of the little finger. Hotteterre (1707, p. 36) says that it should be "placed on the flute between the 6th hole and the molding of the foot." Corrette (c. 1734, p. 25) claims that the little finger is "well extended so that it will always be ready to press down the key." My advice is to ignore the advice of Hotteterre and Corrette. Keeping the hand healthy is a top priority.

Now that the fingers are in place, use this checklist as a guide to using the fingers properly once they are set into motion.

Checklist

- ❏ Keep the fingers relaxed.
- ❏ Raise and lower the fingers "so as not to shake the flute, or produce or communicate any jerk or shock" (Gunn, c. 1793, p. 12).
- ❏ Allow approximately one-half inch between the finger and the open hole. Gunn (c. 1793) recommends lifting the fingers one-half inch above the tone holes. If the finger is allowed to hover too close to its open holes, the pitch of some notes will be flattened considerably and the clarity of the tone impaired.
- ❏ Don't overuse the key. A habit of overuse is sometimes formed when the player attempts to hold the flute more firmly or subconsciously attempts to duplicate Boehm-system flute fingerings. Depressing the key will cause certain notes in the middle range to be quite sharp.

Michel Blavet (1700–1768) was one flutist who actually played the flute left handed; that is, he held the flute to the left, using the right hand to cover the holes nearest the embouchure hole. Try this for fun! It was not, however, a recommended style, even in the eighteenth century. Hotteterre (1707, p. 38) writes:

An Interesting Side Line

> There are others who...hold the flute to the left. I will not absolutely condemn this position of the hands, since you can play as well in this way as in the other, and there would be difficulties in trying to change it. But those who have not yet contracted this bad habit must take care not to fall into it.

ON TONE

And as that Instrument is allowed to be the finest which approaches nearest to the human Voice, the German Flute, from its sweetness and delicacy of Tone, undoubtedly claims a superiority over all others.

Wragg (1792, p. 1)

The tone of the one-keyed flute is quite different from that of the modern Boehm-system flute. We can be guided to an appropriate tone for this instrument (1) by considering the nature of the flute itself, (2) by listening to today's one-keyed flutists, (3) by reading eighteenth-century tutors, and (4) by experimentation.

First consider the nature of the flute itself. The one-keyed flute is designed with a conical bore which is smaller than that of the modern flute. The holes cut for the embouchure and fingers are also smaller. These characteristics are contributing factors to the one-keyed flute's inherently sweeter, quieter, less brilliant sound. Be prepared for these more delicate sounds. One-keyed flutes are made from a variety of materials, which also affect the tone quality. Quantz (1752, p. 50) tells us that a weak tone results from a flute made from porous and light wood, a narrow interior bore, and thin wood; a "thick and masculine" tone requires the opposite features.

Your concept of tone will be rightly influenced by listening to concerts and recordings of today's players of the one-keyed flute. Find good models to imitate, for example, Barthold Kuijken, Wilbert Hazelzet, Stephen Preston, Christopher Krueger, Sandra Miller, Konrad Hünteler, Stephen Schultz, Masahiro Arita, Janet See, and Frans Brüggen. As soon as possible, locate a teacher with whom to study, either privately or by attending master classes.

It is difficult to describe musical sound by way of the written word. However, we can get hints by reading how eighteenth-century flutists described flute tone. Keep in mind that the concept of flute tone undoubtedly differed from player to player and from country to country, even more so than it does today. And concepts changed as time progressed. The quotes that follow are presented in chronological order to give you an idea how the passage of time may have affected the concept of the flutist's tone. The overriding similarity among eighteenth-century sources is that the flute tone should imitate the human voice.

Quantz (1752, p. 50) described the most pleasing tone as one which more nearly resembles a contralto than a soprano and challenged the player to produce "a clear, penetrating, thick, round, masculine, and withal pleasing sound."

Mahaut, writing in 1759 (p. 5), said "the tone is full, round, and clear. It is beautiful when, in addition, [it] is soft, delicate, resonant, and graceful."

Arnold (1787, p. 25) preferred "a full, round, and sonorous tone."

Tromlitz (1791, p. 111) said

> ...the only model on which an instrumentalist should form his tone is a beautiful human voice...one that is bright, full and resonant, of masculine strength, but not shrieking; soft, but not hollow; in short, for me a beautiful voice is full of timbre, rounded, singing, soft, and flexible.

At the end of the century, Gunn (c. 1793) reported conflicting schools of thought regarding tone quality and described two approaches to flute tone. The first stressed a bold, trumpet-like tone, with equal fullness of tone on every note. The second favored a soft tone, a graceful and tender expression with an affinity to the female voice. Gunn himself said that the second method was in some respect correct, but playing exclusively with that tone quality resulted in a monotonous performance. He favored a tone with variety, incorporating as many tone colors as the music demanded.

Finally, experiment for yourself. Be sensitive to the instrument as you play. The flute will help guide you. Ask yourself where the flute speaks and sings at its best.

Several adjustments must be made as a player makes the transition from the modern flute to the one-keyed flute.

Checklist

- ❑ Play without vibrato. (See *On Vibrato* on page 31.)

- ❑ Manipulate the air stream. Experiment with raising and lowering the air pressure, rolling in or out, and adjusting the embouchure to produce the best tone and proper pitch of each individual note.

- ❑ Lower the air speed. You will find that the one-keyed flute, because of its conical bore, doesn't require the player to "drive" the air stream through the tube in the same way the modern flute does. J. Wragg (c. 1792, p. 1) advises that the tone "is not to be acquired by forcing much wind into the Flute, but, on the contrary, by a retention thereof."

- ❑ Some players need to uncover the embouchure hole more than is customary on the modern flute. This can be accomplished in several ways—one being to simply roll the head joint out. Too much coverage deadens the sound. Quantz (1752) says if too much of the hole is covered, the resulting tone will be weak and unclear, but if too little is covered, the tone will be strong, but unpleasant and "wooden."

❏ Experiment with placement. Because the embouchure hole is smaller, it may be helpful to place the flute higher on the lip than you are accustomed to doing on the modern flute. Quantz (1752) recommends placing the inner edge of the blow hole in the middle of the red of the lower lip. Tromlitz (1791) places the flute a little lower—at the point where the red part of the lower lip begins. Experiment to see what works best for you. (To impress your friends, try the placement reported by Mahaut! See the quotation below.)

❏ Lift the fingers. To help assure good tone and pitch, the player may need to lift the fingers higher off the tone holes than for the modern flute. If they are too near the holes, the sound may be flat and less resonant.

❏ Move the fingers crisply. Slow movement may create glides between certain notes.

❏ Expect to produce strong (loud) notes and weak (soft) notes as an inherent part of the character of the one-keyed flute. These light and dark colors are valued, particularly for music of the first half of the eighteenth century. (See *On Homogeneity of Sound* on page 27.)

Quantz (1752), Tromlitz (1791), and others support the use of a flexible embouchure, saying that a gradual and continuous movement of the lips and chin forward is required for notes that ascend. I personally find great benefits in such a flexible embouchure and highly recommend it.

Embouchure

Following Quantz's instructions, the chart below indicates the degree to which the player should cover the embouchure hole for the three d-naturals.

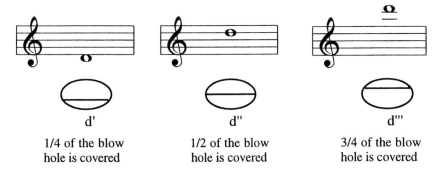

d'	d"	d'''
1/4 of the blow hole is covered	1/2 of the blow hole is covered	3/4 of the blow hole is covered

Mahaut (1759, p. 5) gives us something to chuckle about and to try:

Amusing Side Line

[Some flutists] place the flute between the upper lip and the nose, blowing the instrument from below. This position does not prevent good playing, but it does not look graceful.

ON HOMOGENEITY OF SOUND
(TONE COLOR TENDENCIES)

...good execution must be varied. Light and shadow must be constantly maintained. No listener will be particularly moved by someone who always produces the notes with the same force or weakness and, so to speak, plays always in the same colour...

Quantz (1752, p. 124)

Today's Boehm-system flutist is carefully taught homogeneity of sound— to make the tone color, loudness, and pitch of the scale as equal and consistent as possible. Recall the long hours spent on the Moyse tone studies, striving to create the same color from one chromatic note to the next.[1]

Contrarily, the concept of homogeneity of sound does not apply to early eighteenth-century flute-playing. Part of the beauty the early one-keyed flute is its inherent variety of tone colors; every note has a different character. While color differences are apparent for all one-keyed flutes, those made at the beginning of the eighteenth century have greater tone color differences between the notes than do those from the end of the century.

A goal of early eighteenth-century flute-playing was to find as much variety in color as possible. Each note has its own personality. Some notes are light, some are dark. Some notes are strong, some are weak.

Directly fingered notes are generally strong notes; they ring full and clear. Directly fingered notes are those fingered with no intermittent hole in a line of closed holes. The natural scale of the one-keyed flute is D major, produced simply by beginning with all tone holes closed and opening them in order as shown in the example below. All the notes in the first octave of the D major scale (with the exception of e' if you consider that the hole under the key is closed) are directly fingered, strong notes. Although it can lead to confusion, it is sometimes said that the one-keyed flute is tuned in D.

Strong Notes

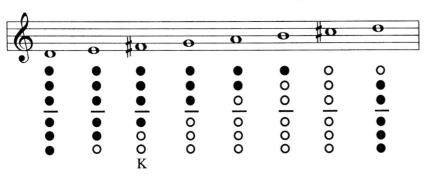

Directly fingered notes are generally strong notes

[1] See Marcel Moyse, *de la Sonorité* (Paris: Leduc, 1934).

Cross-fingered notes are generally weak notes. A cross-fingered note is one in which, instead of all tone holes being closed in successive order, an open tone hole is found intermittently in an otherwise closed line of tone holes. These notes are somewhat veiled and soft. With the exception of e flat in the first and second octaves (produced by adding the key to the d fingering), pitches *not* found in the D major scale are cross-fingered, weaker notes. In the following example, the cross-fingered notes must be played somewhat softly and weakly to maintain the center of the sound and to play the note in tune.

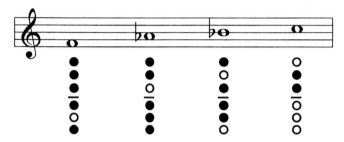

Cross-fingered notes are generally weak notes

Cross-fingered notes lend important distinctive color to the music. And while they are more susceptible to problems of intonation, they can certainly be played in tune with proper adjustments of the embouchure and of the air stream.

Explore the various colors of the one-keyed flute by playing two major scales. The D major scale contains mostly directly fingered, strong notes. Play this scale and observe how the notes speak easily and with strength. The *s* indicates a strong note, and *w* a weak note.

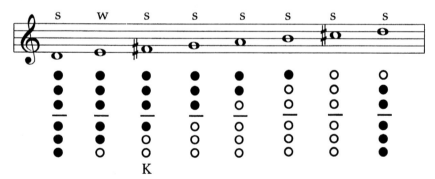

Now play the F major scale. It contains several cross-fingered, weak notes. You will find that not only does the tone color vary from note to note, but the loudness varies as well. It is also more difficult to play this scale in tune. The *s* indicates a strong note, and *w* a weak note.

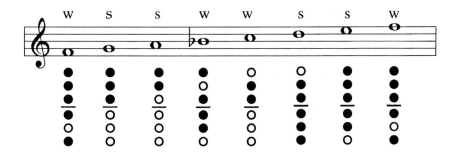

Quantz (1752) said that because of an unavoidable flaw in the structure of most flutes, f natural in the first octave is the weakest note on the instrument.

From playing these two scales, you will observe that tonalities (keys) have different timbres; a scale in D major produces a different timbre than the one in F major. As you play music in different keys, enjoy the individual character of each. The performer should treat this apparent liability as an asset. Listen and learn to appreciate the unique expressive qualities each scale has to offer, for each note within a scale has its own special color characteristic. It is part of the beauty of the one-keyed flute.

By the end of the eighteenth century the concept of a consistent color throughout the chromatic range was taking hold. Flute construction minimized the differences between the notes, and cross-fingered notes came under harsh criticism. (Tromlitz in 1791, [p. 57] declared the cross-fingered g' sharp to be "very dull and dead.") This criticism seems to have occurred about the same time as keys were being added to the flute, which eliminated the distinctive sounds produced by cross-fingered notes.

Changes at Century's End

29

ON KEY (TONALITY)

Pieces set in very difficult keys must be played only before listeners who understand the instrument, and are able to grasp the difficulty of these keys on it; they must not be played before everyone. You cannot produce brilliant and pleasing things with good intonation in every key, as most amateurs demand.

Quantz (1752, p. 200)

D major is the easiest key for the one-keyed flutist. Keys closely related to D major (keys with one and two sharps) are next easiest. The beginner will be wise to select music in D major, G major, or e minor. These are also the tonalities that seem to appear most frequently in eighteenth-century flute literature. Most notes in these keys have a full, clear sound and few awkward cross-fingerings in the usual scale and arpeggio patterns.

The keys farthest away from D major are the most difficult; the farther one strays, the more one will encounter weak notes, intonation difficulties and awkward cross-fingerings. The flat keys (F, B flat, and E flat) are especially challenging. Play the E flat scale in the example below. Half of the notes are weak notes, and half require considerable adjustment for intonation. Three demand cross-fingerings. The arrows indicate whether the pitch of the note must be raised or lowered. The *s* indicates a strong note, the *w* a weak note.

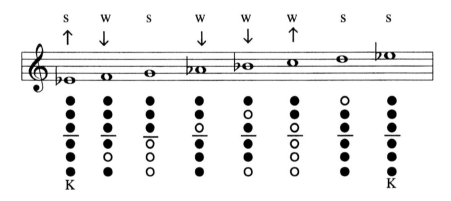

J. S. Bach's *Sonata in E flat* is a very difficult work for one-keyed flute. The beginner should heed Quantz's warning in the quotation above and avoid the difficult keys for a while.

Allegro from Sonata in E flat   J. S. Bach

ON VIBRATO

*A chief beauty of the flute is a firm, clean-cut and even tone;
...[to achieve it] make the chest firm and strong so that it
positively does not shake.*

Tromlitz (1791, p. 215)

The issue of vibrato is a very important one. Should players of the one-keyed flute use vibrato? If so, how should the vibrato be produced?

Today's modern Boehm-system flutist is accustomed to using a throat/diaphragm vibrato as a nearly constant, integral part of the sound. Contrarily, careful study of representative tutors tells us that the tone most recommended for eighteenth- and early nineteenth-century players was probably produced without vibrato. Quantz (1752, p. 162) and others required instead a "clean and sustained execution of the air."

I recommend that the one-keyed flute be played without any vibrato. Because vibrato has become such an integral part of our modern flute technique, some flutists have difficulty playing historical instruments without it. Eliminating the vibrato at first seems cold and lifeless to some. Yet the ear soon accepts the clarity and purity of tone of the one-keyed flute, and eventually the player does not feel the need to rely on vibrato as an important means of expression. Ask what you might do instead. Explore ways to shape and color individual notes. It will become immediately apparent that playing with a straight tone demands good intonation; vibrato cannot be used to cover intonation difficulties, as frequently happens with the modern flutist.

The *Flattement*

An ornament the French called *flattement* (a vibrato-like effect produced with the finger) most closely resembles our modern vibrato.[2] The *flattement* is a wavering of the tone which is slower than that of a trill and produces an interval narrower than a semitone. Instead of fluctuating both above and below the tone (as the modern breath vibrato appears to do), the *flattement* produces a fluctuation with a pitch *lower* than the given tone.

modern vibrato   *flattement*

Unlike modern vibrato, the *flattement* was used sparingly and reserved for long notes.

[2] This ornament was known by many names. In France it was called *flattement* or *tremblement mineur;* in Germany, *Bebung;* in Italy, *tremolo;* and in England "softening," "close shake," or "lesser shake." Today, fingered vibrato is most often referred to by its French name, *flattement.*

31

To produce the *flattement* the player taps the finger several times in succession on the edge of the first open tone hole (being careful not to cover the hole completely), or fully on a further removed hole, in a manner similar to that of producing a trill. These two methods produce a difference in the intensity of expression. For example, to produce *flattement* for g', one may tap the finger on the edge of the fourth hole, or open and close fully the fifth hole. The *flattement* is terminated with the finger lifted from the hole.

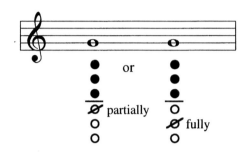

According to Tromlitz (1791), the undulation of the *flattement* can be uniform, or it can increase or decrease in speed.

Uniform speed	Speed increases	Speed decreases

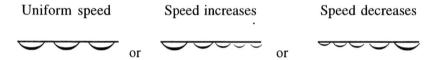

Lindsay (1828–30, p. 30) preferred that the *flattement* begin slowly, then become faster as the note fades away "until, at last, the vibration ceases, as if from extreme exhaustion, and the sound faintly expires upon the ear."

Tromlitz (1791, p. 215) made it very clear that the *flattement* was not akin to a breath vibrato when he wrote, "I remind you once again that on the flute the *flattement* may not be made with the chest, because if it is one can very easily get into the habit of wobbling, which results in a miserable execution."

Flattement is used on long notes, probably most often in slow movements. Hotteterre (1707) tells us that *flattement* is used frequently on whole notes, half notes, and dotted quarter notes.

By the end of the century, it was used with less frequency. Tromlitz (1791) said it could be applied to long notes, fermatas, and to the note before a cadence, but that it was used infrequently. Two years later, Gunn (c. 1793, p. 18) expressed a real dislike of the ornament, saying it is "inconsistent with just intonation, and not unlike that extravagant trembling of the voice which the French call *chevrotter*, to make a goat-like noise, for which the singers of the Opera at Paris have been so often ridiculed." By the time Gunn published his tutor, the *flattement* was just one of many ornaments falling out of use.

On long notes, the *flattement* is often accompanied by a crescendo and decrescendo. The Italian term *messa di voce* is used to identify this practice of swelling and diminishing long notes.

The *Flattement* with the *Messa di voce*

To perform an effective *messa di voce* with the *flattement,* Quantz (1752) instructs us to "begin pianissimo, allow the strength of the tone to swell to the middle of the note, and from there diminish it to the end of the note in the same fashion, making a vibrato with the finger on the nearest open hole." Follow Quantz's instructions as you play the following notes.

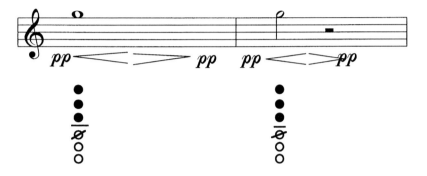

Although the *flattement* was seldom notated, Hotteterre, Philidor, Prelleur, Corrette, and Delusse are among a handful of composers who did notate it, however sparingly, in their music. The sign was placed over the head of the note to be ornamented.

Notation

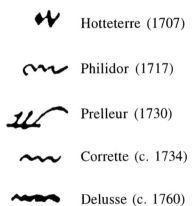

Hotteterre (1707)

Philidor (1717)

Prelleur (1730)

Corrette (c. 1734)

Delusse (c. 1760)

The truth of the matter is, breath vibrato *was* used by some flutists in the eighteenth century. We know that is the case because it was the subject of criticism on the part of several flutist/writers. In order for there to be a platform for criticism, we must assume that it was practiced.

Are We Certain that Breath Vibrato Was Not Used?

The French tutor by Delusse (c. 1760, p. 9) is the only eighteenth-century flute tutor of nearly one hundred I examined which recommends producing vibrato with the breath. Delusse writes that it should be used as often as possible and produced "by an active movement of the lungs only while puffing the syllables *hou, hou, hou.*"

Most tutors do not mention breath vibrato at all. Several criticized its use, among them tutors by Geminiani and Tromlitz. Geminiani (c. 1747) tells the reader that the violin may vibrate any note whatsoever, but is careful to point our that the flutist must reserve the *flattement* for long notes. Tromlitz (1791, p. 214) states firmly that vibrato is not done with the breath and claims it "makes a wailing sound, and anyone who does it spoils his chest and ruins his playing altogether."

I refer you to Catherine Parsons Smith, *Characteristics of Transverse Flute Performance in Selected Flute Methods* (1969) for a study of vibrato in the eighteenth and early nineteenth centuries. Betty Bang Mather, *Interpretation of French Music from 1675 to 1775* (1973), provides a good summary of what early tutors had to say about the *flattement*. See the annotated bibliography for complete entries.

Recommended Readings

See page 97 for a *flattement* chart for the one-keyed flute.

ON INTONATION

...the transverse flute still retains some degree of estimation among gentlemen, whose ears are not nice enough to inform them that it is never in tune.

Sir John Hawkins (1776, Vol. II, p. 739)

Players of the modern Boehm-system flute sometimes describe their first encounter with the one-keyed flute as a love-hate relationship. On the positive side, the flutist is enthralled by its expressive, mellow tone, the feel of the wooden instrument in the hands, and the vibrating air column under the fingers. However, it becomes immediately apparent that the instrument is capable of being played badly out of tune. The intonation is affected by the most subtle movements of the fingers, the air pressure, and the embouchure.

Eighteenth-century flutists found the flute easy to play out-of-tune as well. Tromlitz (1791) felt that the flute was perhaps the most difficult of all instruments to play in tune. He thought that the natural unevenness of the tone, blowing too hard or too softly, an incorrect embouchure, improperly tuned flutes, and the placement of the holes in positions to accommodate the fingers, were all contributing elements.

However, the flute can be played in tune if great care is taken to listen and to adjust. Quantz (1752, p. 55) believed that a good ear, among other things, can help overcome problems of intonation:

> It is true that the flute has certain imperfections in several chromatic keys. This defect can be easily remedied, however, if the player possesses a good embouchure, a good musical ear, a correct system of fingering, and an adequate knowledge of the proportions of the notes.

Gunn (1793, p. 1) also believed that the fault lay primarily with the player, not with the flute. He answered critics like Hawkins (see quotation above) by referring to "the number of performers who play it perfectly in tune; this objection could only have arisen from hearing it in very imperfect hands."

Tuning is a complex subject. Haynes[3] (1991, p. 357) writes that "playing 'in tune' is a relative and personal affair...it depends so much on context." The subject cannot be covered adequately in a book as concise as this one, but you may find what follows of some help—instruction on how to tune, a discussion of what it means to play "in tune," an introduction to enharmonically equivalent notes, and suggestions on the practical application of this material.

---

[3] One of the most accessible references for tuning systems for non-keyboard instruments is an article by Bruce Haynes, "Beyond temperament," *Early Music,* 19: 3 (August 1991), 357-381.

The first requirement is to put the flute in tune with itself. Begin by tuning the second octave d natural to a fixed pitch (electronic tuner or keyboard). Quantz (1752) tells us that the majority of players in his day tuned to this note. You may pull or push the head joint to adjust the overall pitch of the flute, but Quantz warns not pull out the other joints or the intonation of the entire flute will go awry.

Next, Quantz recommends tuning the three d naturals to one another. Move the cork to facilitate the tuning (see page 6 for specific instruction).

Quantz (1752) tells us that the inner bore of the one-keyed flute must be constructed so that the upper octaves are a little sharp. To correct this problem, he recommends blowing the sharper notes in the second and third octaves more weakly, at the same time covering more of the blow hole with the lower lip. Conversely, blowing the flatter notes in the first octave more strongly and drawing the lips back will raise the pitch.

The following exercise (from Corrette's flute tutor [c. 1734]) with its wide leaps, requires the use of this method. (You'll find fingerings on p. 63.)

Prelude in Octaves   Michel Corrette

The modern flutist might be mildly shocked when first picking up the one-keyed flute because some notes at first seem remarkably "out of tune." Let's use f sharp (in both the first and second octaves) as an example—many players who come from a modern flute experience comment on the seemingly "flat" f sharp. Where this note *is* often somewhat flat, it may not be as flat in its musical context as your tuner might suggest. How can this be?

Most modern flutists use equal temperament as the primary reference for tuning. The one-keyed flutist will no doubt encounter and use a larger range of temperaments than the modern flutist. So first be aware that most modern electronic tuners, such as the popular Korg tuner, are tuned in equal temperament.[4] Knowing where the notes are in equal temperament is a valuable reference, so using an electronic tuner is a good idea. But as the American traverso player Christopher Krueger says, the Korg has its dangers—what looks good on a Korg may not necessarily sound good in the context of eighteenth-century music. He finds the Korg tuner useful as a drone for practicing pure intervals in different keys.[5]

But back to our example. The proper pitch of any note is subject to more than the temperament one is using—the harmonic function of the note is also a critical factor. A good flutist will adjust the pitch of a note depending on its function in a given key. For example, the player will on many occasions play f sharp lower in pitch than an equal-temperament tuner demands. When f sharp functions as the third in D major, it is lower in pitch (and appears "flat" on the tuner) than when it serves as the fifth of b minor.

Most eighteenth-century tuning systems differentiate between half-steps, according to their harmonic function, and subsequently the player must treat enharmonically equivalent notes as separate pitches.

Enharmonic Notes

Those notes with sharps are lower in pitch than their counterparts with flats. For example, g' sharp and a' flat are considered to be different notes and different pitches, g' sharp being considerably lower in pitch.

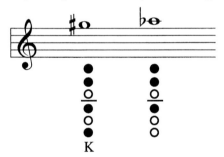

G sharp is lower in pitch than A flat

While there are numerous such enharmonic pairs, the flutist comes across only four with any degree of regularity. Give your attention to Ab/G#, Bb/A#, Eb/D#, and Db/C#. In each set the first note (the note with a *flat)* is higher in pitch than the second (the note with a *sharp).*

Enharmonically equivalent notes were treated as separate pitches throughout the eighteenth century.[6] References to this can be found from the

---

[4] Korg has a newer (but costly) model called the MT-1200 multi-temperament tuner that allows the player to select a temperament and key with which to tune.

[5] Personal communication, September 1997.

[6] In the nineteenth century, the treatment of enharmonic notes began to reverse itself. Tutors by the two leading French flutists, Louis Drouet (London: R. Cocks & Co., 1830) and Jean-Louis Tulou (Mainz: Schott, 1853), tell us that *notes sensibles,* or leading tones (the enharmonic notes with sharps) are higher in pitch than their equivalent enharmonics (notes with flats).

first tutor for the one-keyed flute (Hotteterre, 1707) to late eighteenth-century tutors by Tromlitz (1791) and Gunn (c. 1793). Quantz (1752, p. 46) went so far as to design a two-keyed flute (one key for d sharp and a second key for e flat) because "the e flat must be a comma higher than d sharp." He discusses this two-keyed flute in his tutor, but says although it had been around since about 1726, it did not catch on.

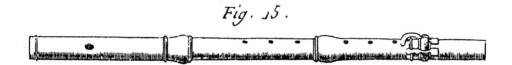

Fig. 15.

Quantz's Two-Keyed Flute

Illustration from an engraving designed to illustrate an article on Quantz's flutes in Vol. III (1777) of the *Supplément* to Diderot's *Encyclopédie*. Illustration reproduced in Reilly's translation of the Quantz tutor, *Johann Joachim Quantz: On Playing the Flute.*

Talk of temperaments and enharmonically equivalent notes as separate pitches can be confusing. What is a practical way of handling this information responsibly? Christopher Krueger feels that perhaps Vallotti & Young temperament (No. 8) found on the Korg MT-1200 tuner is the best compromise for late baroque music in general. This temperament would look something like the chart below on an **equal-tempered** electronic tuner. In explanation, -6 means that the note f sharp will appear 6 cents "flat." If, while using an equal-tempered electronic tuner, the sweep needle shows the following variations, you are "on track," doing well! I chose the D Major, A Major, G Major, and e minor scales because they are the keys represented in the tunes in this book.

Practical Application

D Major Scale		A Major Scale		G Major Scale		e minor Scale	
d'	+2	a'	0	g'	+4	e'	-2
e'	-2	b'	-4	a'	0	f#'	-6
f#'	-6	c#'	-8	b'	-4	g'	+4
g'	+4	d"	+2	c'	+2	a'	0
a'	0	e"	-2	d"	+2	b'	-4
b'	-4	f#"	-6	e"	-2	c'	+2
c#'	-8	g#"	-6	f#"	-6	d#"	-4
d"	+2	a"	0	g"	+4	e"	-2

What does this mean? Depending on circumstances—harmony, temperament, and perhaps what simply "sounds good"—you may be moving away from equal-temperament tuning (the standard set by your tuner) by as much as, or more than, the increments shown on this chart. For example, you may be playing f sharp 6-cents "flat" (by equal-temperament standards) but be playing "in tune" with your colleagues. Although the chart above represents only one temperament, perhaps it is a good place to begin.

Tuning is indeed a complex issue that depends on context, sound, and blend. Playing frequently with others is the best way to learn to play the one-keyed flute with a good sense of the proportion of the pitches, so play often with other musicians, especially in the beginning stages of your development. Gunn (c. 1793) recommends playing with string players, keyboard players, or with an accomplished flutist to help cultivate the ear, and Quantz (1752, p. 114) tells the player to "constantly direct his ear to those who play with him."

Practicing Good Intonation

The experienced Boehm-system flutist makes microscopic adjustments for proper intonation. Now a new set of adjustments must be learned for the one-keyed flute, for a given note will not have the same pitch tendencies on both the one-keyed flute and modern flute. The written instructions that accompany the Complete Fingering Chart on page 65 will tell you when a given note tends to be sharp or flat, and how to adjust its pitch.

Adjusting for Intonation

The following checklist gives special attention to the skills already possessed by the proficient modern flutist. One can make many adjustments to correct intonation on the one-keyed flute, some of them quite different from those made on the Boehm flute. At first, try these adjustments one at a time—the goal is to become comfortable with them so they will soon be working in harmony with one another.

❑ Roll the flute in and out. Hotteterre (1707), Quantz (1752), and Tromlitz (1791) are among those eighteenth-century flutists who recommend turning the flute in and out to correct faulty intonation. At least one well-known professional player today does this successfully by flexing the left wrist. I personally find that this method makes the flute feel unstable and prefer instead to make embouchure adjustments and manipulate the air stream.

❑ Make embouchure adjustments. An active embouchure is an important component in playing in tune. Use those methods that work for you on the modern flute, including raising or lowering the air stream, covering more or less of the embouchure hole with the lower lip, making the aperture larger or smaller, and raising or lowering the head. In part because of its small embouchure hole, the one-keyed flute responds quickly to these embouchure adjustments.

❑ Manipulate the air stream. Make necessary pitch adjustments by increasing or decreasing the air flow. Experiment with a faster or slower air stream. Work more with the air stream than you are accustomed to doing on the modern flute to make adjustments. (You will find instruction for specific notes on the Complete Fingering Chart on page 65.) Weak and strong notes will result from increasing or decreasing the air flow, but this is an expected, valued component of the flute sound, just as it was during the first part of the eighteenth century. (See *On Homogeneity of Sound* on page 27.) Modern flutists are traditionally not accustomed to making the kind of air flow adjustment required for the one-keyed flute, but you should make a concerted effort to do so.

❑ Experiment with alternate fingerings to correct intonation. (See the Complete Fingering Chart on page 65.)

❑ Check the finger height: Gunn (c.1793) recommends that the fingers be lifted one-half inch above the tone holes; if they are nearer, the sound is flat and less clear. This is an important point. Modern flutists are commonly taught to keep the fingers very near the keys, but that technique can cause intonation problems on the one-keyed flute. To test this theory, play c sharp with the unused fingers close to the tone holes, then again with the fingers one-half inch above the holes, and notice the difference.

❑ Pulling the head joint out more than one-eighth inch (about three millimeters) will begin to affect the overall response of the flute. This is because the wall of a wooden flute is very thick and pulling the head joint excessively will create a "canyon" at the tenon.

❑ Memorize the intonation tendencies of the one-keyed flute and make the necessary adjustments before you play the note. The ear must be constantly alert.

ON PLAYING *FORTE* AND *PIANO*

This waxing and waning is part of the making of light and shade,
and consequently of good performance.
Tromlitz (1791, p. 234)

The one-keyed flute is beautifully expressive in its capacity to respond to subtle nuances. Its dynamic range is more limited than that of the modern flute, but those subtle changes that are available to the player are an important feature of expressive playing. Quantz (1752, p. 110) tells us that "playing always on the same level would soon become tedious."

The one-keyed flute plays *piano* easily, but does not have the *forte* power of a modern Boehm flute. You'll find that a crescendo produced as you would on the modern flute will distort the tone and pitch of the one-keyed flute; the one-keyed flute simply doesn't respond favorably to being pushed by the air stream.

Alternatively, you will find that a full, well-centered tone will produce the desired *forte* you are searching for. Further, it is important to maintain this concept of a well-centered tone throughout the dynamic range.

To produce soft notes, Quantz (1752) recommends that the player moderate the wind (use a slower air speed), then turn the flute outward as needed to correct the pitch. To produce loud notes, strengthen the wind (use a faster air speed) and turn the flute inward.

Quantz also suggests that if one wishes to play more softly for a movement such as an Adagio, the screw cap may be used to temporarily press the cork plug in toward the embouchure hole for the entire movement.[7] This adjustment makes the sounding length of the flute shorter, the pitch of the flute higher, and helps keep the flutist from playing flat. The beginner might do well to save experimenting with the screw cap in this manner for a later time.

Using the Screw Cap

---

[7] One must have a device called a screw cap on the end of the flute for this to work. See page 7 for a description of the screw cap.

ON RHYTHMIC HIERARCHY

The length and shortness of sounds has many degrees in music of which poetry knows nothing, and more variety yet comes from the many time signatures.

Mattheson (1739, p. 170)

Not all beats are created equal in eighteenth-century music. Some beats are strong, some are weak, depending on where they fall within the rhythmic framework. It is impossible to make generalizations about all music in regard to which beats are strong and which are weak. However, several seventeenth- and eighteenth-century writers have left us with instruction which might be organized into a metric grid—a grid that might serve as a spring-board from which to organize our music. First a word about "good" notes and "bad" notes.

Strong beats and weak beats produce "good" notes and "bad" notes. Think of notes on strong beats as being "good" notes; play them longer and a bit louder. Think of notes on the weak beats as being "bad" notes; play them shorter and a bit softer. Muffat (1698) explains these two types of notes:

> "Good" Notes
> "Bad" Notes

> ...there are those that are good, and others that are bad. Good notes...are longer ones, those that come on the beat or essential subdivisions of measures, those that have a dot after them, and (among equal small notes) those that are odd numbered and are ordinarily played down-bow. The bad notes are all the others, which like passing notes, do not satisfy the ear so well, and leave after them a desire to go on.[8]

The writer of an eighteenth-century keyboard tutor, Daniel Gottlob Türk (1789, p. 88–104), explains that the first note of a bar in common time is "good" or strong; it is the longest and loudest. The third note is also good, but not as good as the first. The second and fourth notes are "bad" or weak; they are shorter and softer. Play the following series of quarter notes—the dynamic markings are Türk's way of showing which notes are stronger and louder. The sign *pf* stands for poco forte, the marking midway between *f* forte and *mf* mezzo forte. The difference in length and loudness should be subtle, but should also create rhythms that are supple and swinging.

Italian Peasants (excerpt from page 151)

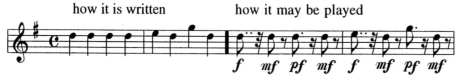

8 See Houle, "Meter and Performance," *Historical Performance,* 2:1 (Spring 1989), 12, for transl.

The following system of notation from Türk, using dashes and arches, is helpful in showing this rhythmic hierarchy:

The first of the following charts, based on Türk's instructions, shows how the strong and weak beats fall in two-part meters.

In three-part meters the first beat is the strongest. The third beat is usually next strongest, but occasionally it is the second beat.

Should the player apply this strong-note, weak-note structure to all musical situations? Definitely not. Many musical influences will superimpose themselves upon this metric grid. The stress may be shifted, for example, to express harmony, bring out a dissonance, shape a phrase, or acknowledge a cross-rhythm. Türk tells us that there are a variety of single tones which receive emphasis, regardless of where they fall within the metric structure— among them are appoggiaturas, syncopated notes, notes which create dissonance, and tones distinguished by their length, and highness or lowness. One might choose to use the metric structure outlined on the charts above as a point of departure, but there will be many musical reasons to shape the performance otherwise. As I said before, you may use Türk's ideas as a metric grid from which to organize the music, but be prepared to make many exceptions to the grid.

Practical Application

43

What are quick notes? They are usually sixteenth notes, but sometimes eighth notes or quarter notes, depending on the meter. Quantz (1752) identifies the sixteenth note as the usual quick note in common time, 2/4, 6/8, and 3/8 meters. In cut time and 3/4 meter, the eighth note is normally the quick note; in 3/2 time, usually the quarter note. He makes a point of adding that these are the quick notes only as long as still more rapid notes are not intermingled.

Quick notes have a metric framework similar to that of larger metric structures as described above. Quantz tells us that the first, third, fifth, and seventh notes of a quick-note group are the "good" quick note and must be played slightly longer and stronger than a "bad" ones—the second, fourth, sixth and eighth. The strengthening and lengthening of quick notes will also be subtle.

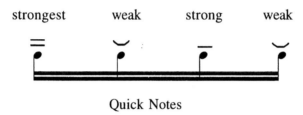

Quick Notes

Musicians today normally beat time (tap the foot) on every beat —more than once per bar. Contrarily, many seventeenth-, eighteenth-, and nineteenth-century writers teach us that the foot generally beats (hits the floor) only once per bar, on the first beat of the measure. This downbeat is followed by only one upbeat per bar.

Beating time in this way gives us one more tool in making rhythmic hierarchy come to life. We can feel the strong and weak beats in our large muscular system.

How does this method of beating time work? Following are examples in duple and triple meter. The arrow down indicates the downbeat, when the foot hits the floor; the arrow up indicates the upbeat, when the foot is in the air. Play these examples as you beat time.

1. **Duple Meter** (Common time, Cut time, 2, 2/4, 6/4, 6/8, and 12/8) In duple meter the upbeat occurs halfway through the measure, dividing it into two equal parts.

Prussian March (excerpt from page 118)

44

2. **Triple Meter** (3/2, 3/4, 3, 3/8, and 9/8) The eighteenth-century dancing-master Kellom Tomlinson (1735, pp. 147–8) writes that in triple meter the foot (1) comes down on beat one, (2) rests on the floor on beat two, and (3) is raised in readiness for the next measure on beat three. The flute method by Vanderhagen (c. 1800) offers similar instruction. The downbeat therefore is twice as long as the upbeat. One might count "**one**-two-**three**," making the first note the most important, third note next most important, and the second note least important. Again, the arrow down indicates the downbeat, when the foot hits the floor; the arrow up indicates the upbeat, when the foot is in the air.

Grazioso (excerpt from page 169)

The minuet is a dance in triple meter; the minuet step takes two measures to complete. Tomlinson (1735) teaches us that the foot comes down on the first measure and comes up on the second measure. Try this for the minuets in this method book.

Minuet (excerpt from page 118)

Primary sources for the study of rhythmic hierarchy and meter include Daniel G. Türk, *Klavierschule* (1789) and Leopold Mozart, *Versuch einer gründlichen Violinschule* (1756). See also George Houle, "Meter and Performance in the Seventeenth and Eighteenth Centuries," *Historical Performance* (1989); Houle cites another primary source—Georg Muffat, *Florilegium Secundum* (1698). See also Claire A. Fontijn, "Quantz's *unegal*: implications for the performance of 18th-century music," *Early Music* (1995).

To learn more about beating time, see the following two secondary sources: Arnold Dolmetsch, *The Interpretation of the Music of the XVIIth and XVIIIth Centuries* (1915) and Robert Donington, *The Interpretation of Early Music* (1992). Donington quotes primary sources by John Playford (*Introduction to the Skill of Musick.* London, 1654), Christopher Simpson (*Compendium of Music.* London, 1665), and Jean Rousseau (*Methode Claire.* Paris, 1678). Another important primary source is Kellom Tomlinson, *The Art of Dancing* (1735). Also see flute tutors by Amand Vanderhagen (c. 1800), Thomas Lindsay (1828–30), and Charles Nicholson (1836). See the annotated bibliography for complete entries.

Recommended Readings

ON ARTICULATION

---

*...it takes a hard-working person who is not put off by any effort
to learn to play with correct articulation.*

Tromlitz (1791, p. 210)

An understanding of articulation practices is essential to playing eighteenth-century music in its true spirit. Articulation brings wonderful, subtle nuance to the music; it is the architect for phrasing and rhythm. There are many articulation options available to the one-keyed flutist that are not indicated in the printed score. It is both necessary and rewarding to accept the responsibility of learning to play the one-keyed flute with stylistic articulation. First, let us explore articulation silences.

There are numerous occasions when the player must play a note shorter than it is notated, thereby creating a small silence. In the eighteenth-century the particular application of these silences was governed by "good taste."[9] On the flute, the silence can be created with the help of the tongue. Quantz (1752) instructs the flutist to achieve this "articulation silence" with the articulation *tu*—an articulation silence is produced when the tongue returns to the palate and stops the sound (as in *tut*).[10] These articulation silences are particularly abundant in Allegro movements,[11] and the result is a mix of long notes (notes held their notated value) and shortened notes (notes played shorter than their notated value), which help the player express the rhythmic hierarchy, clarify rhythmic and melodic figures, and bring out important notes. According to Quantz, it was in good taste to apply articulation silences to the following situations. The dotted lines indicate where the silence occurs.

Articulation Silences

---

[9] See Michel de Saint-Lambert, *Les Principes du Clavecin* (Paris, 1702), transl. Carol MacClintock, *Readings in the History of Music in Performance* (Bloomington: Indiana University Press, 1979), 222–23. Saint-Lambert describes an ornament called the *détaché*, which creates a small silence between two notes. Its application is appropriate to many musical situations (before trills and mordents, for example) and is a matter of good taste. François Couperin describes a similar practice called an *aspiration* in his keyboard tutor *L'Art de toucher le Clavecin* (Paris, 1716).

[10] Quantz (1752, 217–219) instructs the violinist to use a detached bow-stroke to create the silence.

[11] See C.P.E. Bach, *Essay on the True Art of Playing Keyboard Instruments* (1753), transl. William J. Mitchell (London: Cassel, 1951), 149. Bach tells us that in general Adagios are expressed by broad, slurred notes and Allegros by detached notes.

1. Between repeated notes, so that two notes on the same pitch may be heard clearly and distinctly.

Prussian March (excerpt from page 118)

Italian Peasants (excerpt from page 151)

2. Between leaps when they are formed by eighth notes in the Allegro.

Delightful Pocket Companion (excerpt from page 159)

3. After syncopated notes.

Air by Mr. Weideman (excerpt from page 126)

4. After dotted notes.

Air by Mr. Weideman (excerpt from page 125)

5. Before trills, mordents, and appoggiaturas. The articulation silence makes them seem to be stressed.

La Belle Catherine (excerpt from page 112)   Minuet (excerpt from page 116)

6. Before one or more shorter notes that follow a longer note.

Prussian March (excerpt from page 118)

Eighteenth-century music is full of both slurred notes and tongued notes. While it is clear how to handle slurred notes (notes connected under one uninterrupted breath), questions arise about how to perform the tongued notes. If the composer has not indicated a particular articulation, the player may choose a special eighteenth-century tongue stroke pattern for quick notes.

Unslurred Notes

The most common eighteenth-century articulation syllables for quick notes are *tu* (or *ti*) and *ru* (or *ri*); English-speaking flutists may find it easier instead to think of them as *tu* (or *too*) and *du* (or *doo*). Incorporating an infinite variety of articulation patterns using these syllables into the music is great fun! Once eighteenth-century articulation patterns are understood, the player may no longer feel compelled to play Allegro movements with lightning speed. Instead, alternating *tu du* patterns can be used for the quickest notes, resulting in an Allegro that swings and rollicks with great energy. What a welcome relief from the often-heard "sewing machine"— rigidly even—quick notes.[12]

Eighteenth-
Century Patterns
for Quick Notes

The notes eligible for *tu du* tonguing patterns are usually the quick notes (sixteenth notes or eighth notes). These notes must move in *stepwise* motion (or sometimes leap by an interval of no more than a third) and not fall under a slur. Quick notes are grouped in pairs by alternating tongue strokes—*too'-du* or *tu-doo'*. The syllables *too'* and *doo'* are longer and stronger, *tu* and *du* are shorter and weaker.

Notes are frequently grouped in two-note patterns. The examples below indicate only two of many performance possibilities—both produce rhythmic and musically interesting results.

1. First, the quick notes may be grouped within the pulse in a strong-weak (or long-short) grouping using *too'-du.* This grouping mimics the poetic meter called *trochaic* verse.[13] For example, the childhood poem *Mar' y had' a lit' tle lamb'* has a strong-weak pattern similar to the bracketed sixteenth notes in the example below.

[12] See Sol Babitz, *The Great Baroque Hoax* (Los Angeles: Early Music Laboratory, 1970) for an opinionated but entertaining reference on rhythm.

[13] See John Gunn, *The Art of Playing the German-Flute* (London, c. 1793), 24–26 for a discussion of poetic meter as it relates to flute-playing.

Allegro from Sonata in G Major   Händel

2. Or, the quick notes may be grouped across the beat in a weak-strong (or short-long) grouping using *tu-doo'*. This grouping mimics the poetic meter called *iambic* verse. The lyrics to the childhood song *Bingo* has a weak-strong pattern similar to that in the musical example below. *There was' a far'mer had' a dog'*. The brackets show the two-note groupings.

Allegro from Sonata in G Major   Händel

Double Tonguing

A broad variety of double-tongue patterns were used by eighteenth-century flutists—*doodle, deedle, diddle,* and *tootle* to name a few. Many tutors of the period recommended using these patterns for the quickest notes in the fastest movements. The first syllable is made like the normal *doo* or *too* attack. The second is produced by releasing the air at the sides of the tongue after the tip of the tongue has returned to the palate. Learning this articulation can be postponed until a later time. Meanwhile, the modern double-tongue syllables *du-gu,* which you may already know, have a nice flow and will produce about the same result.

Recommended Readings

The above examples will help you get started. There are many more articulation syllables and patterns to explore. Invest the time to read the chapters on articulation in the flute tutors by Quantz (1752), Tromlitz (1791), and Hotteterre (1707); Tromlitz devotes 52 pages to the subject. I also recommend *Solfeggi pour la flute traversiere avec l'enseignement, par Monsr. Quantz* (1978), which contains articulation examples as recommended to Frederick the Great by his teacher J. J. Quantz in the mid-eighteenth century—you'll find this music listed in Appendix B. Claire A. Fontijn's article "Quantz's *unegal*: implications for the performance of 18th-century music," *Early Music* (1995) is a good companion article to the *Solfeggi*. Fontijn translates those portions relating to *inégal* and identifies some of the musical excerpts. Betty Bang Mather's *Interpretation of French Music from 1675 to 1775 for Woodwind and Other Performers* (1973) is a helpful, easy-to-understand contemporary resource for French articulation practices. See also Mather's *Dance Rhythms of the French Baroque* (1987). Bruce Haynes's article "Tu ru or Not Tu ru...,"*Performance Practice Review* (1997) looks at tonguing syllables for transverse flute as found in tutors dating 1700–1827. See the annotated bibliography for complete entries.

While reading about articulation is valuable, nothing suffices like hearing a good example. Listen to recordings of today's leading traverso players. Find opportunities to work with a qualified teacher and study eighteenth-century articulation practices with an experienced player.

ON FURTHER READINGS

Our best sources for study of the one-keyed flute are the many flute tutors published from 1707 to the mid-nineteenth century. I strongly recommend that the serious player invest the time to read primary sources, especially the important flute treatises from the eighteenth century. The earliest treatise is by Hotteterre (1707); the best-known work is by Quantz (1752). Refer to the survey in Appendix A for my list of the "Top 13" tutors from the eighteenth century. Most in foreign languages on this list are available in English translation. Most are also available in facsimile edition. They are readily accessible, so there is no excuse not to seek them out and do some reading.

The following early music periodicals will also be of interest:

1. *Traverso.* A quarterly newsletter devoted exclusively to historical flutes. Edited by Ardal Powell. Published by Folkers & Powell, 49 Route 25, Hudson, NY 12534. Includes listings of new books and articles, and compact disc recording releases. A great way to stay in touch.

2. *Early Music.* A quarterly magazine published by Oxford University Press (England). The February 1995 issue is devoted to the flute—featured are articles on articulation, improvisation, the flutes of Denner, musical iconography, Quantz, and flutists known to J. S. Bach. The ads are informative too. Look for advertisements about instrument makers (especially those making modern replicas of one-keyed flutes), publishers (to learn about facsimile editions and new urtext editions), and recording companies (for new releases). *Early Music* reflects largely the European scene via its ads and articles on festivals and concerts.

3. *Early Music America.* Join the organization called Early Music America (11421 1/2 Bellflower Road, Cleveland, OH 44106) and receive both its quarterly publication *Early Music America* (which is a great way to stay current on what is happening in the United States) and a monthly newsletter (which lists, among other things, performances by early music groups throughout the United States).

The Internet offers a growing number of listings related to historical flute-playing. Search for web sites on the Internet with a "web crawler" such as those found at www.yahoo.com or www.lycos.com or www.excite.com. Many web sites include links to other sites with similar or related information.

CHAPTER III

FINGERINGS FOR THE ONE-KEYED FLUTE

Illustration by Piccard from Antoine Mahaut,
Nieuwe manier om binnen korten tyd op de Dwarsfluit te teeren speelen. /
Nouvelle méthode pour apprendre en peu de tems à joüer de la flûte traversière.
Second edition. Amsterdam: J. J. Hummel, c. 1759.

ON FINGERINGS

To achieve any degree of perfection in your playing, you must combine good playing with a thorough knowledge of both the strengths and weaknesses of your instrument, to be able to correct the intonation whether with the embouchure or with fingering.

Mahaut (1759, p. 8)

Why So Many Choices?

A glance at the Complete Fingering Chart on page 65 will show the reader that there are far more fingering choices for a given note on the one-keyed flute than for the modern flute. One set of fingerings (as represented on the Basic Fingering Chart on page 63) cannot in good conscience be applied to all one-keyed flutes. The flutes themselves vary so—each differs in bore size, tone hole size, and tone hole placement. According to James (1826), a flute with a large bore and large tone holes must have different fingerings than one with smaller holes and a smaller bore.

The player must choose fingerings to complement the flute being played. Ask your flute maker which flute he or she copied. For example, if your flute is a modern replica of the so-called Hotteterre flute (French flute from the early eighteenth century), you may wish to refer to the charts in Hotteterre's *Principes* (1707). More importantly, the player must listen carefully and observe how the instrument responds to a particular fingering.

Lowering the Pitch

A given pitch on the one-keyed flute can be lowered by closing additional holes farther down the tube of the flute. The method works by lowering pitches a semitone. In the following example, g' sharp is produced by first fingering a', skipping one tone hole, then closing holes until the desired pitch is reached.

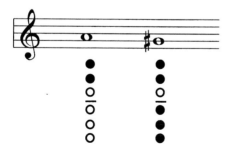

Using the same approach, pitches can be lowered to correct faulty intonation. For example, a' sharp can be lowered by adding fingers of the right hand. Play the following example:

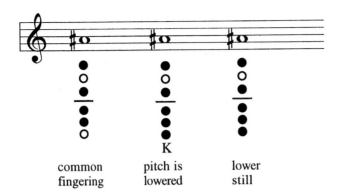

common fingering   pitch is lowered   lower still

When playing in the first two octaves, you may discover that by resting the little finger on the key (and subsequently opening the hole), the fingerings seem more like those of the modern flute and the flute may seem more secure in your hands. Try each of the following notes, first without the key, as indicated on the fingering chart, then with the key depressed.

Use of the Key

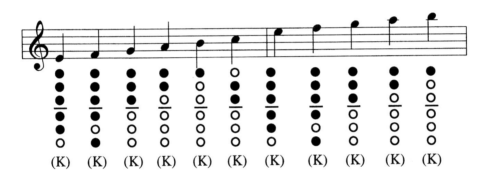

You will discover that although the flute may feel more secure with the key depressed throughout the passage, the pitches of e', e", f', and f" are raised substantially and are not acceptable. The pitches of the other notes are not adversely affected, however.

Two conflicting schools of thought existed in the eighteenth century regarding the extensive use of the key. Although the charts do not show the use of the key on those notes where the pitch is adversely affected, what is to be done with those notes (like g, a, and b) where pitch is not an issue? Mahaut (1759) says that on several notes in the first two octaves, it does not matter whether the key is open or closed. But Quantz (1752) did not use the key on these notes and cautioned the student not to fall into the habit of allowing the little finger to remain on the key because of the intonation problems this practice creates.

How may we solve this dilemma? I recommend that in general you follow Quantz's recommendation and avoid overusing the key. Use the key only as recommended on the Basic Fingering Chart on page 63. If the intonation is not adversely affected, however, you may consider making exceptions, such as the two I propose below.

1. Quick passages. Where a note is preceded and/or followed by one which uses the key, the player may be able to keep the key down through the entire passage.

2. Trills. Where more stability is desired to hold the flute, the player may be able to keep the key down throughout an entire passage without adversely affecting the intonation, as in the example below.

Extending the Range

As stated earlier, the easy range of the one-keyed flute is first octave d' to third octave e'''. For the sake of simplicity, I recommend that the beginner limit his or her first efforts to this easier range. During the first part of the eighteenth century, notes higher than e''' were usually avoided. Later in the century, we find more high notes. Mahaut (1759, p. 7) lists fingerings for a''' through d'''', but says that they are "only obtainable on *flutes d'amour* or bass flutes, though some ordinary flutes can reach as high as b''' natural."

On some eighteenth-century fingering charts, there appears at the bottom of the range, a low c' sharp, produced artificially by fingering d' and rolling the flute in. (See the Complete Fingering Chart on page 65.)

Alternate F Sharp

Alternate fingerings for f' sharp and f'' sharp merit explanation. The common fingerings for these notes are somewhat flat. Alternate fingerings for f sharp, which raise the pitch significantly, are shown below.

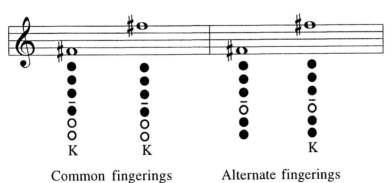

Common fingerings   Alternate fingerings

57

Quantz (1752) recommends using the alternate f sharp when it lies next to g sharp or e sharp, both of which are slightly high in pitch. The alternate f sharp is a weaker note, but its higher pitch matches the notes around it. Play the following examples.

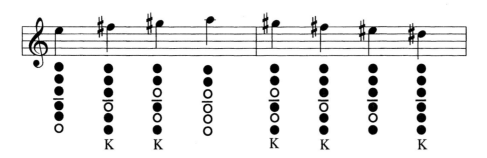

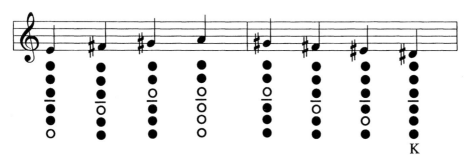

Quantz (1752) says this alternate f sharp is used more in slow movements and cantabile passages (where the pitch is more discernible) than in fast movements. The use of the alternate f sharp is discontinued when the music modulates; Quantz says (1752, p. 45) "when the g sharp becomes g, you must use the regular f sharp again, at first sounding it a little higher than usual, until the ear is again accustomed to it."

How Many Fingerings

There are a great many fingerings to choose from. How many alternate fingerings should one learn and incorporate into one's playing? That becomes a personal choice. Tromlitz (1791, p. 62) chose to limit the number of fingerings in his repertoire, saying that complications can arise:

> I am not fond of many fingerings for the same note, for none of them is quite the same as the others, but always a little lower or higher, and each requires its own approach; they only make complications, and one does not acquire any certainty.

ON TRILLS

If an instrumentalist or singer were to possess all the skill required by good taste in performance, and yet could not strike good shakes [trills], his total art would be incomplete.

Quantz (1752, p. 101)

You'll probably enjoy playing ornaments on the one-keyed flute because of the instrument's great agility. Trills are often easier on the one-keyed flute than on the Boehm flute; there are no cumbersome keys to negotiate and the flute responds quickly to delicate gestures.

Trill fingerings require special attention. They are sometimes different than you would expect them to be, and the resulting sounds are also sometimes different than you would expect. Be careful not to subject the one-keyed flute to preconceived ideas and Boehm-system fingerings.

Wide Trills

You will quickly become aware that many trill fingerings listed by eighteenth-century sources do not produce "true" tones and semitones. In the first part of the eighteenth century, a preferred trill was often a wide semitone interval; these trills may sound sharp to modern ears. The wide intervals create a lively, brilliant trill.

For example, the e to f sharp trill is not played using the customary f sharp fingering (1 2 3 / 4 _ _ K), but by using a fingering which produces an intentionally wide trill.

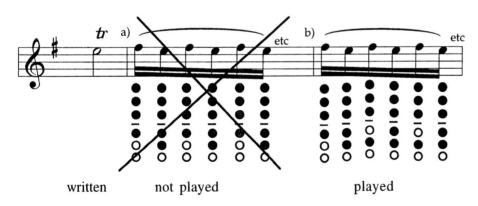

written   not played   played

By the late eighteenth century, the idea of wide trills was changing. Tromlitz (1791, p. 248) writes that the e to f sharp trill using the fourth finger, as in the correct example above, is an "old error, and it has been preserved without thought of anything to replace it." Tromlitz instead recommends trilling with the fifth finger, as in the "incorrect" example above.

59

Some late eighteenth-century flutists were making an effort to minimize the wide trills with adjustments of the breath and fingers. Gunn (c. 1793, p. 18) suggests that in the following example, the player must "suppress the tone as much as possible, and by lifting up the finger to the least possible distance above its hole …[make] the B as flat as possible," otherwise a b natural sounds:

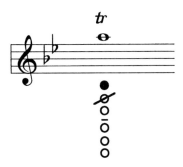

Trills in eighteenth-century music begin most often with the upper neighbor and are placed on the beat, creating a dissonance with the underlying harmony. The following example is one way you may choose to execute a cadential trill:

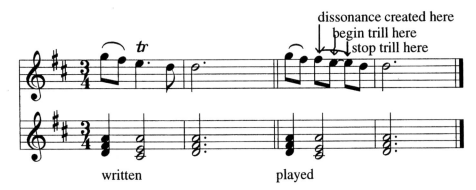

Gunn (c. 1793, p. 18) gives the following advice for executing the trill.

> …keep the flute and the tone very steady, while the finger making the shake is to come down to its hole with a smartness, like the stroke of a hammer, and instantly to rebound again to its former place, and being rather more solicitous about this, and always making its motions in regular time, than about making them very quick, which will naturally follow.

In response to our modern training, we Boehm-system flutists often feel the need to trill for the full duration of the ornamented note. However, eighteenth-century trills are not so rigid, and there are actually many other possibilities. Experiment with trilling only the first part of the note to be ornamented; often a couple of finger jiggles will suffice.

The following example shows an abbreviated trill. I like to call such a trill a "double jiggle"—although this is **not** eighteenth-century terminology, it is descriptive.

According to Quantz (1752, p. 101), trills must not be played so fast that the ear cannot distinctly hear two separate pitches.

Recommended Readings

I recommend the following three secondary sources for further study of the trills in eighteenth-century music: Betty Bang Mather, *Interpretation of French Music from 1675 to 1775 for Woodwind and Other Performers* (1973) and Frederick Neumann, *Ornamentation in Baroque and Post-Baroque Music* (1978). Also see Chapter Eleven, "The Trill" in Ardal Powell, *The Virtuoso Flute-Player...*, a translation of Tromlitz's 1791 flute tutor. See the annotated bibliography for complete entries. See Margaret Neuhaus, *The Baroque Flute Fingering Book* (1986) for a trill chart compiled from several eighteenth-century tutors.

You'll find trill fingerings arranged in the form of studies by eighteenth-century author Lewis Granom on page 79.

EXPLANATION OF THE CHARTS

Four fingering charts follow. The first is a Basic Fingering Chart containing the most frequently found fingerings. The most frequently encountered enharmonic fingerings are included.

The second chart is the Complete Fingering Chart containing all fingerings found for each chromatic note, with the enharmonic spellings intact, just as they appeared in eighteenth-century tutors. I have given instruction, as found in historical tutors, for the embouchure adjustments required to play each note with good pitch.

The third is not so much a trill chart as a trill exercise. It comes from Lewis Granom, *Plain and Easy Instructions for Playing on the German-Flute* (London, c. 1770) and was selected because it is the most detailed collection of trill fingerings for the one-keyed flute to appear in any eighteenth-century tutor. However, only one option is given for each note. For a chart that compiles trill fingerings from a number of sources, see Margaret Neuhaus, *The Baroque Flute Fingering Book* (1986).

The fourth chart is a *Flattement* Chart that shows how to produce fingered vibrato.

The fingerings in the charts that follow come from my "Top 13" flute tutors dating 1707 to 1793 (see Appendix A). I first compiled these charts in 1979 for a class I taught in conjunction with the Coe Baroque Flute Workshop at Coe College, but they have not been published until now.

BASIC FINGERING CHART
FOR THE ONE-KEYED FLUTE

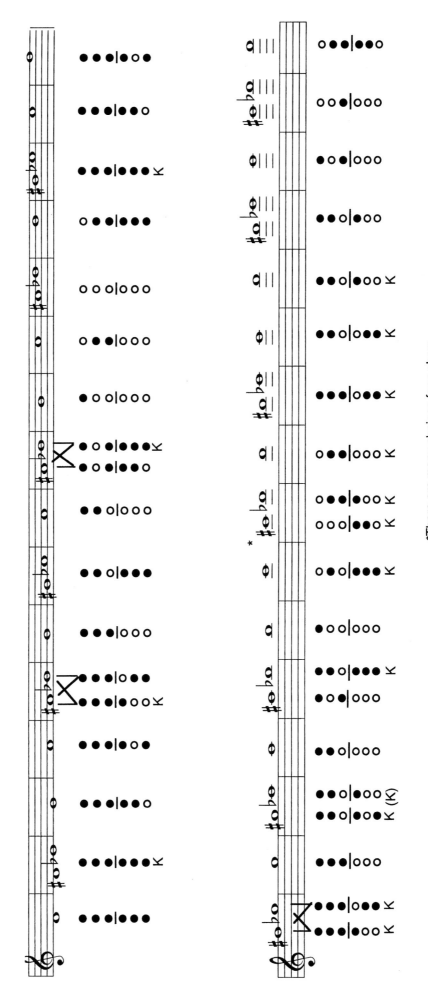

*There are many choices for c sharp.
See the Complete Fingering Chart.

63

COMPLETE FINGERING CHART

…[as] each flute is tuned differently, a single system of fingering cannot be suitable for all flutes.

Tromlitz (1791, p. 53)

The following chart is a compilation of those charts found in the "Top 13" eighteenth-century method books for the one-keyed flute (see Appendix A). *Fingerings* are listed in order of the frequency with which they were found—the first fingering listed was encountered most often, the last, the least often. *The letter K* on the chart below refers to the key: depress the key when *K* is included on the chart. *Comments* refer the reader to the fingering with of the same number and come from written instructions found in the list of "Top 13" eighteenth-century tutors.

A word about enharmonic fingerings. Enharmonic fingerings have distinctive pitches and specific fingerings are given to achieve those pitches. (see *On Intonation* on page 35). Some tutors make a distinction between the enharmonics (Hotteterre, Delusse, Prelleur, Quantz, Mahaut, Tromlitz, and Gunn). On these charts, a sharp is lower in pitch than b flat, c sharp is lower than d flat, and g sharp is lower than a flat, and so on. Quantz (1752) says the notes with flats are a comma higher than those with sharps. Other writers make very little or no distinction at all (Corrette, Granom, Heron, Vanderhagen, and Devienne).

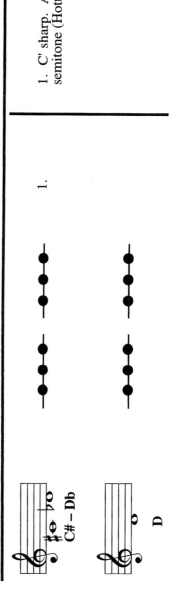

1. C' sharp. An artificial note. Turn the flute in enough to produce a semitone (Hotteterre).

65

2. E♭ flat. Usually a little low in pitch. Vanderhagen recommends tightening the lips a little and blowing more forcefully.

3. E' natural. Usually a little low in pitch. Vanderhagen recommends tightening the lips a little and blowing more forcefully. Tromlitz cautions the player not to open the key; that will make the note too sharp.

4. F' flat. Eighteenth-century tuning systems called for a distinction between f flat and e natural. Lip f flat up a little, making it sharper than e natural.

5. F' natural. High in pitch. Quantz declares this to be the weakest note on the flute. Turn the flute in by lowering the head a little to flatten it (Hotteterre). Turn the flute in, moderate the wind, and advance your upper lip a little (Quantz). Mahaut says it is better to correct with the embouchure, enlarging the opening of the lips slightly so that the upper lip comes forward a little. Heron says this note will always be a quarter tone too sharp without care; correct it by making the embouchure opening larger. Vanderhagen also recommends correcting the pitch with the embouchure: make the aperture larger and advance the upper lip. Tromlitz warns never to use the key.

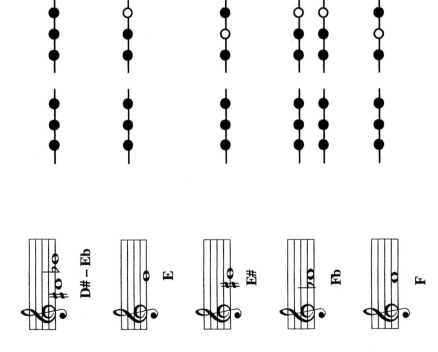

6. F♯ sharp: Low in pitch. Tromlitz declares this note to be low on all flutes. Turn the flute out and raise your head a little (Hotteterre). Rotate the flute out or strengthen the wind (Quantz & Tromlitz). Vanderhagen recommends tightening the lips a little and blowing more forcefully. Be sure to use the key.

7. F♯ sharp. High in pitch. Moderate your wind and turn the flute in (Quantz). Quantz considers this a good choice for use in passages containing e sharp and/or g sharp.

8. G♭ flat. High in pitch. Turn the flute in (Hotteterre). Mahaut says it is better to correct with the embouchure, enlarging the opening of the lips slightly so that the upper lip comes forward a little. Hotteterre says that g′ flat is different (higher in pitch) than f′ sharp, both in this octave and in the next: not enough people make this distinction.

9. G′ natural. A good note. Tromlitz recommends using the key to make it brighter and stronger, then correcting the resulting high pitch with the embouchure. Most of his colleagues disagree and don't use the key.

10. G′ sharp. High in pitch. Turn the flute in to adjust it (Hotteterre). Vanderhagen recommends making the aperture larger and advancing the upper lip. Gunn says to blow it very softly or it will have a very dull and bad sound. Tromlitz declares it dull and dead: blow it gently.

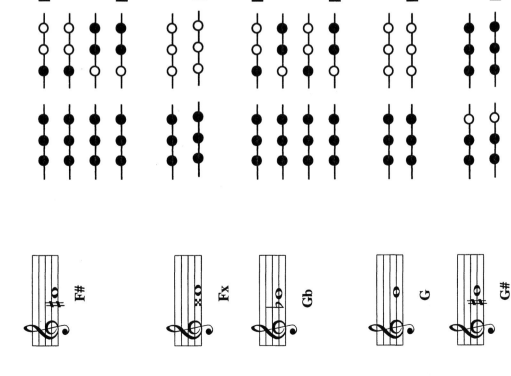

11. A' flat. High in pitch. Turn the flute in, but not as much as for g' sharp, because a' flat is higher in pitch than g' sharp.

12. A' sharp. High in pitch. Turn the flute in, or try another fingering (Hotteterre). Vanderhagen recommends making the aperture larger and advancing the upper lip. Tromlitz declares this a dull, weak note: blow it softly. A sharp should sound lower in pitch than b flat.

13. A' sharp. This fingering brings the pitch down a lot.

14. B' flat. High in pitch. Moderate the wind. Mahaut shows this fingering used in quick, leaping passages. Gunn says to blow it very softly or it will have a very dull and bad sound.

11.

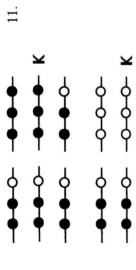

12.
13.

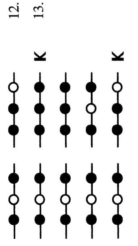

14.

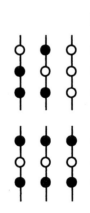

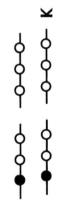

15. C" flat. Quite low in pitch. Rotate the flute perceptibly out (Quantz). Mahaut says some people turn the flute out but it is better to correct with the embouchure by drawing the lips back toward the corners of the mouth and slightly increasing the breath.

16. C" natural. Gunn says to blow it very softly or it will have a very dull and bad sound.

17. C" natural. High in pitch. Hotteterre tells us that several people finger c" natural in this way, but he does not recommend it because it is too high in pitch.

18. C" sharp. Quite low in pitch. Turn the flute out by as much as you can (Hotteterre & Quantz). Heron says to correct it by making the embouchure opening larger.

69

15.

16.

17.

18.

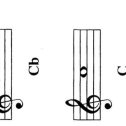

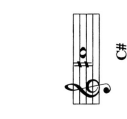

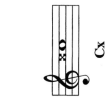

19. D″ flat. Low in pitch. Mahaut says some people turn the flute out, but it is better to correct with the embouchure by drawing the lips back toward the corners of the mouth and slightly increasing the breath.

20. E″ flat. Low in pitch. Turn the flute out a lot so that this semitone is higher in pitch than d″ sharp (Hotteterre). Mahaut says some people turn the flute out but it is better to correct with the embouchure by drawing the lips back toward the corners of the mouth and slightly increasing the breath.

21. E″ natural. Tromlitz cautions never to use the key; it is a bad habit that is very frequently encountered.

22. F″ flat. This semitone should be higher in pitch than e″ natural. Quantz and others support adding the key, which raises the pitch.

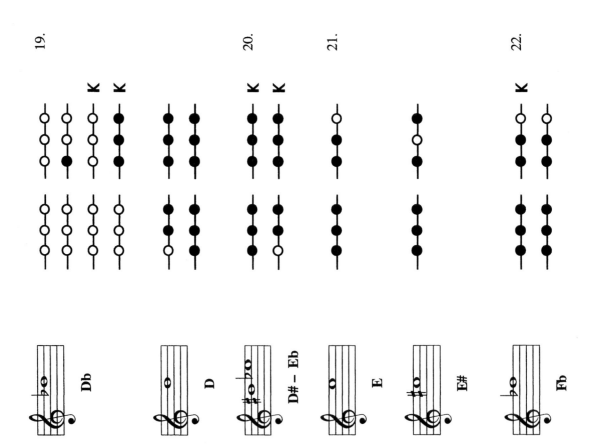

23. F" natural. High in pitch. Turn the flute in (Hotteterre). Turn the flute in and moderate the wind (Quantz). Heron says this note will always be a quarter tone too sharp without care; correct it by making the embouchure opening larger. Vanderhagen also recommends correcting the pitch with the embouchure: make the aperture larger and advance the upper lip. Tromlitz warns never to use the key.

24. F" sharp. Low in pitch. Tromlitz declares this note too low on all flutes. Turn the flute out and raise your head a little (Hotteterre). Heron says to make the embouchure opening larger. Vanderhagen recommends tightening the lips a little and blowing more forcefully. Be sure to use the key.

25. F" sharp. Low in pitch. Rotate the flute out or strengthen the wind.

26. F" sharp. High in pitch. Moderate your wind and turn the flute in (Quantz). A good choice for passages containing g" sharp and/or e" sharp. Quantz says this fingering is used more in slow, cantabile passages than in quick ones.

27. G" flat. High in pitch. Hotteterre declares this fingering to be the best, but that it must be adjusted by turning the flute in a lot. He further states that g" flat is used very little...only in highly chromatic passages.

23.

F

24.

25.

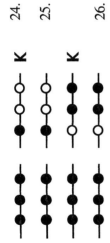

F#

26.

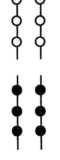

Fx

27.

Gb

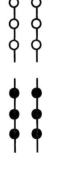

G

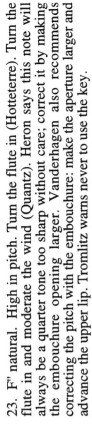

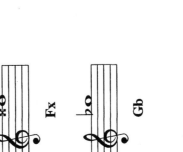

28. G" sharp. High in pitch. Moderate your wind and turn the flute in (Quantz). Vanderhagen recommends making the aperture larger and advancing the upper lip to lower the pitch.

29. G" sharp. High in pitch. Turn the flute in (Hotteterre).

30. A" sharp. High in pitch. Turn the flute in (Hotteterre) and moderate the wind (Quantz). Vanderhagen recommends making the aperture larger and advancing the upper lip to lower the pitch.

31. B" flat. Mahaut says to use this fingering when b" flat is preceded or followed by c'".

32. B" flat. You must turn the flute out to make a difference between a" sharp and b" flat; the latter should be higher in pitch (Hotteterre). On some flutes, depressing the key may facilitate this effort.

72

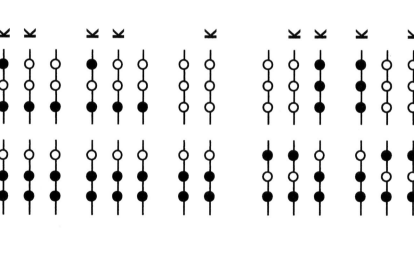
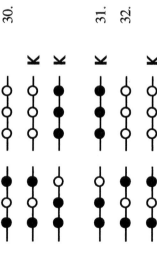
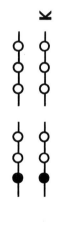

33. C''' natural. Hotteterre says that this note is high on some flutes and low on others, and is delicate to adjust. If it must be lowered, blow more softly and turn the flute in; another alternative is to half stop the sixth hole. If it must be raised, then use the alternate fingering _ _ 3 / _ 5 6 [which is the last fingering on the list at the left]. See explanation number 34 below.

34. C''' natural. An alternate fingering should the c''' natural listed first on this chart prove to be too low in pitch.

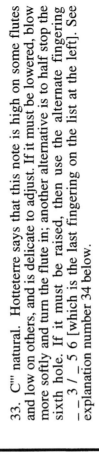

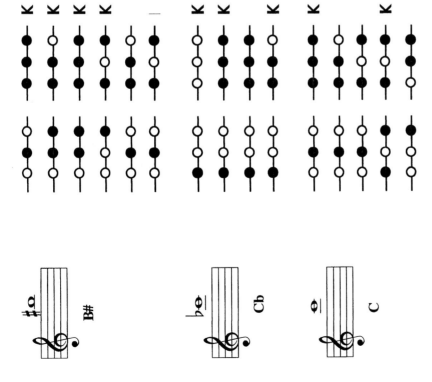

33.

34.

B#

Cb

C

35. C''' sharp. High in pitch on many flutes.

36. C''' sharp. Low in pitch.

37. C''' sharp. Low in pitch. Turn the flute out (Hotteterre).

38. C''' sharp. This alternate fingering lowers the pitch of the first c''' sharp on this chart. Quantz says it is possible only where the movement is slow, and recommends its use when c''' sharp follows b'' sharp (b'' sharp fingered - 2 3 / 4 5 6 K).

39. C''' sharp. Mahaut says to use this fingering only to prepare the cadence or trill on b'' natural.

40. D''' flat. Should be higher in pitch than c'' sharp.

41. D'''. Sometimes high. Turn the flute out (Hotteterre). Hotteterre says this note is difficult to adjust.

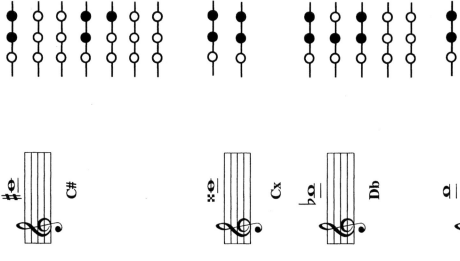

42. D'' sharp. Sometimes high.

43. E''' natural. Somewhat flat. Turn the flute out and sustain your breath well (Hotteterre).

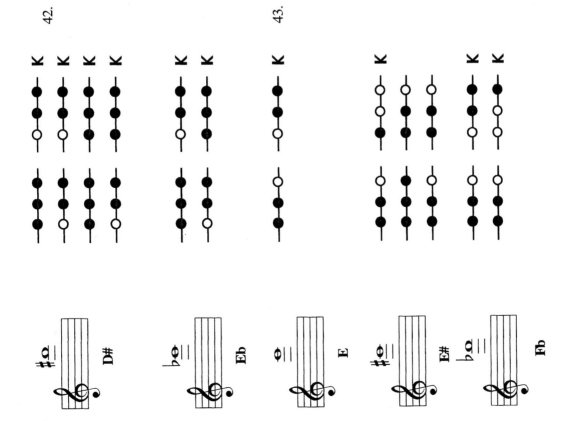

44. F''' natural. Hotteterre declares that f''' natural can almost never be played on the flute. He gives this fingering and suggests the flutist blow very strongly.

45. F''' natural. Mahaut declares that this fingering makes this problematic note playable on most flutes, but a little tricky to get because of the partially closed first hole.

46. F''' sharp. A little high in pitch on some flutes. Mahaut says to correct the pitch by turning the embouchure in a little.

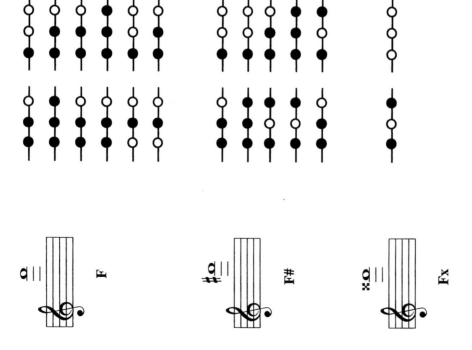

76

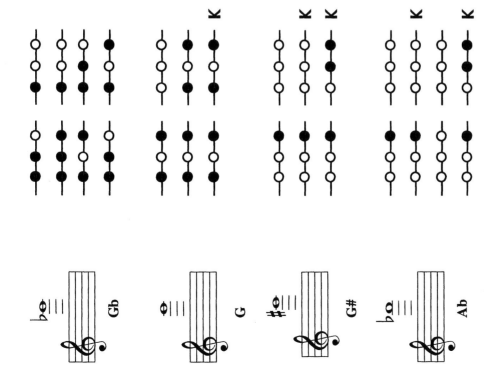

47. A''' was considered by most eighteenth century flutists to be the highest usable note. Some charts show fingerings beyond this a'''. However, these highest notes almost never appear in the music.

47.

TABLE OF TRILLS

Since the trill is one of the most splendid ornaments, but also one of the most difficult...it is important to try with unceasing and tireless diligence to learn it.

Tromlitz (1791, p. 236)

The following facsimile (unchanged reprint) is a table of trill fingerings is found in Lewis Granom, *Plain and Easy Instructions for Playing on the German-Flute* (c. 1770, p. 121–138). Granom's work is reprinted here because it is the most complete table of trills to be found in an eighteenth-century flute tutor. The trills all begin from the upper neighbor—Granom calls it the "preparatory note"—and each trill has a close, or "resolution."

The following table contains black and white dots. You must stop the holes with your fingers when you see a black dot and leave the holes unstopped when you see a white one. The bottom-most hole on the fingering chart represents the hole covered by the key. This may be a bit confusing at first, but realize that when this dot is black, the key is *not* depressed; when it is white, the key *is* depressed. Some dots are half black and half white; in that case, the holes they represent must be half-stopped.

The trills are organized by key. Most major and melodic minor scales are represented. Each note the scale is given with its trill fingering. While this format may make it more cumbersome to find a particular fingering, it does allow the student to make an exercise of the trill fingerings. Scales don't necessarily begin on the first degree; sometimes they begin at the bottom of the range of the flute. Occasionally you will see *Refer to No. 1* or *Refer to No. 2*, etc.—Granom is referring the reader to trill fingerings for notes found in *natural* minor scales (see facsimile pages 137–38).

No one set of trill fingerings is equally useful for every flute and every situation. Perhaps some of these fingerings will not work for you. I refer you to Margaret Neuhaus, *The Baroque Flute Fingering Book* (1986) for a compilation of fingerings from twenty-one sources.

79

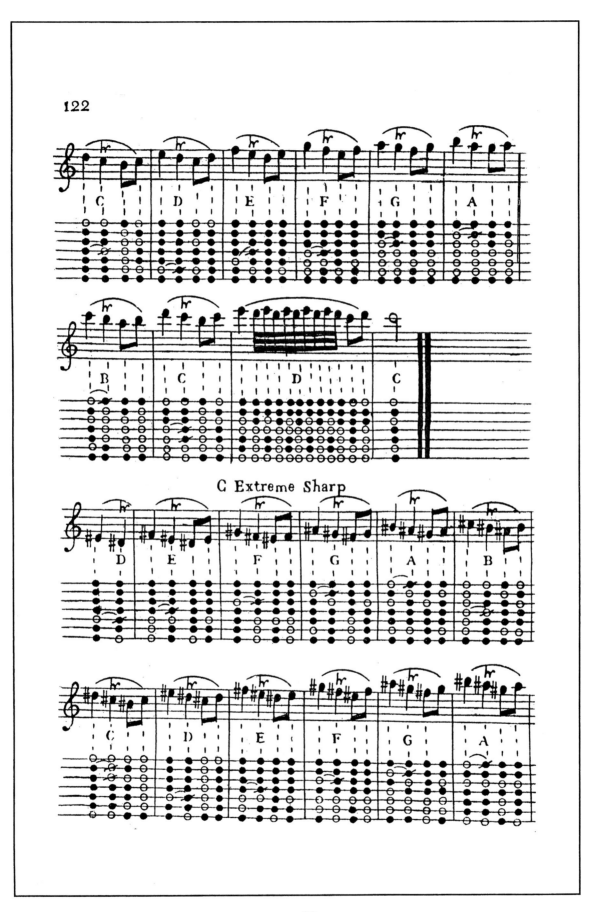

122

C Extreme Sharp

C SHARP MAJOR

80

C MINOR

A Sharp by Flats

D Flat

Refer to No

A FLAT MAJOR

D MINOR

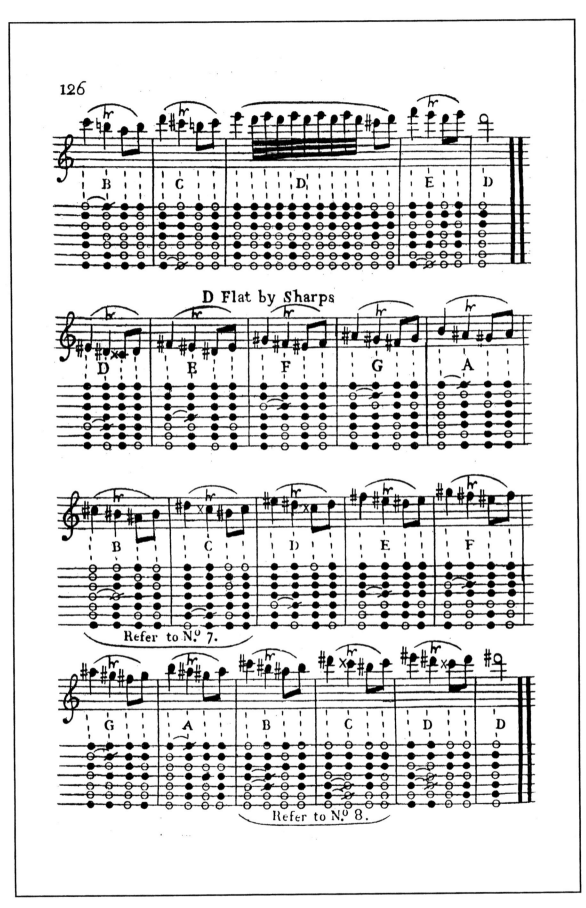

D Flat by Sharps

Refer to Nº 7.

Refer to Nº 8.

D SHARP MINOR

D MAJOR

E MINOR

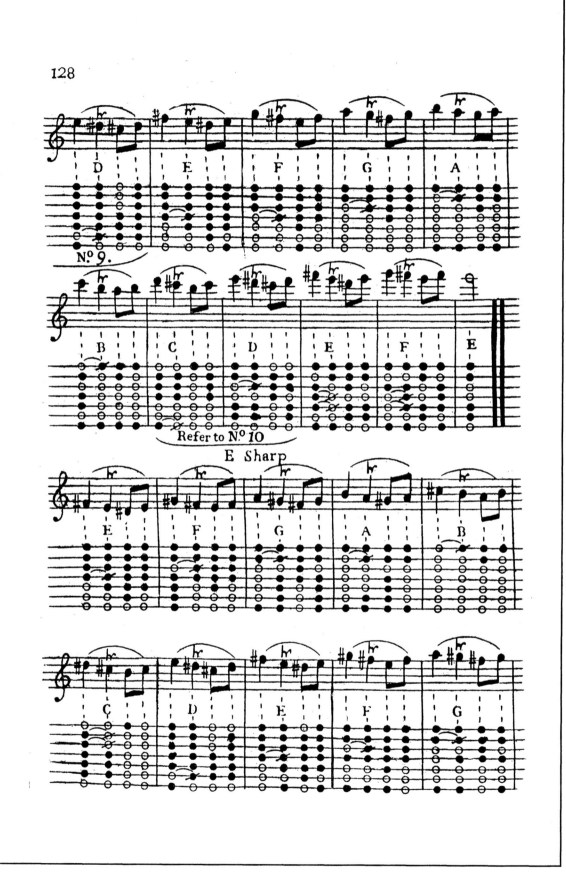

E MAJOR

E Sharp by Flats

E FLAT MAJOR

129

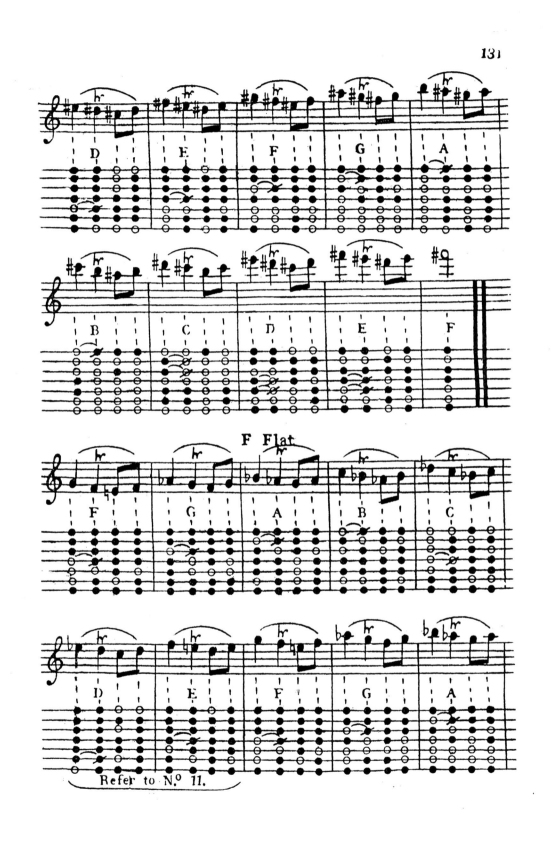

F MINOR

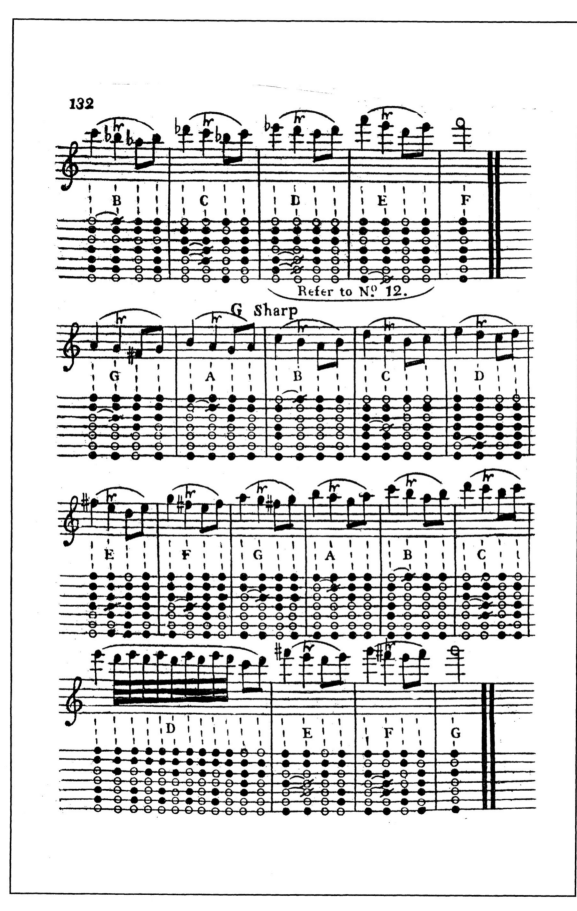

135

B Sharp

B MAJOR

93

B Flat by Sharp

B MINOR

Refer to Nº 15

Refer to Nº 16

A Scale, of fuch Shakes, as are found in all flat Modes defcending; inverted from the other Scale.

REFERENCES FOR NATURAL MINOR SCALE PATTERNS

FLATTEMENT CHART

Being of an extremely delicate character, the Vibration—like the Glide—should only be applied to passages of great fervour and sensibility; but when so introduced, the effect is truly sweet and beautifully expressive. It should, however, be sparingly employed.

Lindsay (1828–1830, p. 30)

The following *flattement* chart was compiled from instruction and charts in the tutors by Hotteterre, Corrette, Tromlitz, and Mahaut (see Appendix A). Refer to *On Vibrato* on page 31 for a discussion of the *flattement* (fingered vibrato).

*	Begin and end the note with the tone hole (indicated by the arrow) fully covered.
↓e	Touch the finger on the edge of the tone hole.
↓f	Cover the tone hole fully with the finger.
shake flute:	Imitate *flattement* by shaking the flute with the right hand. Some notes present special problems because all the fingers are being used to stop the holes.

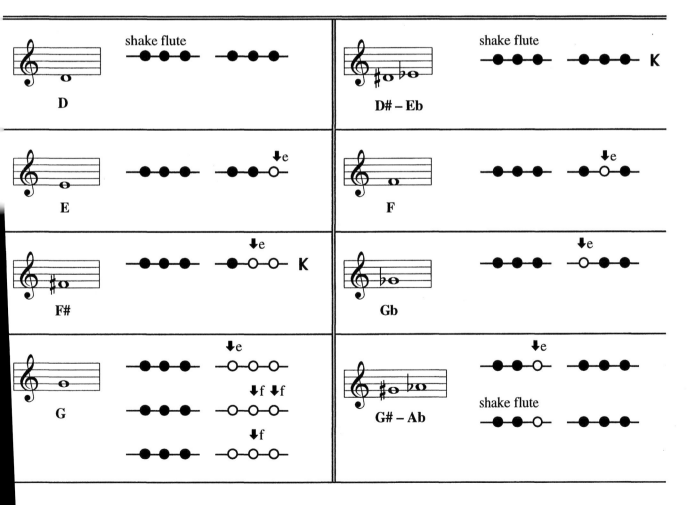

97

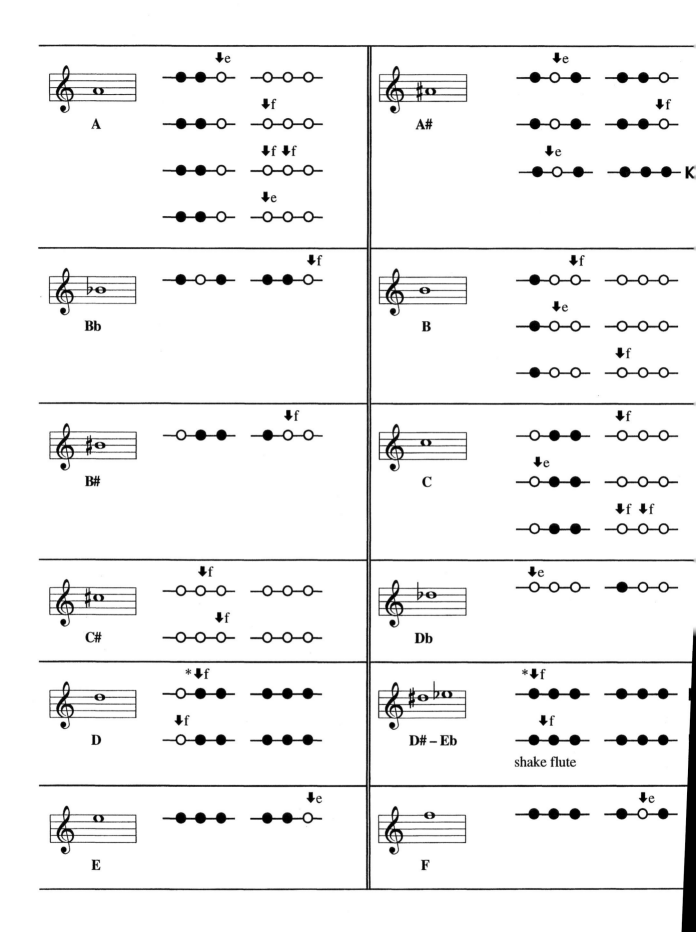

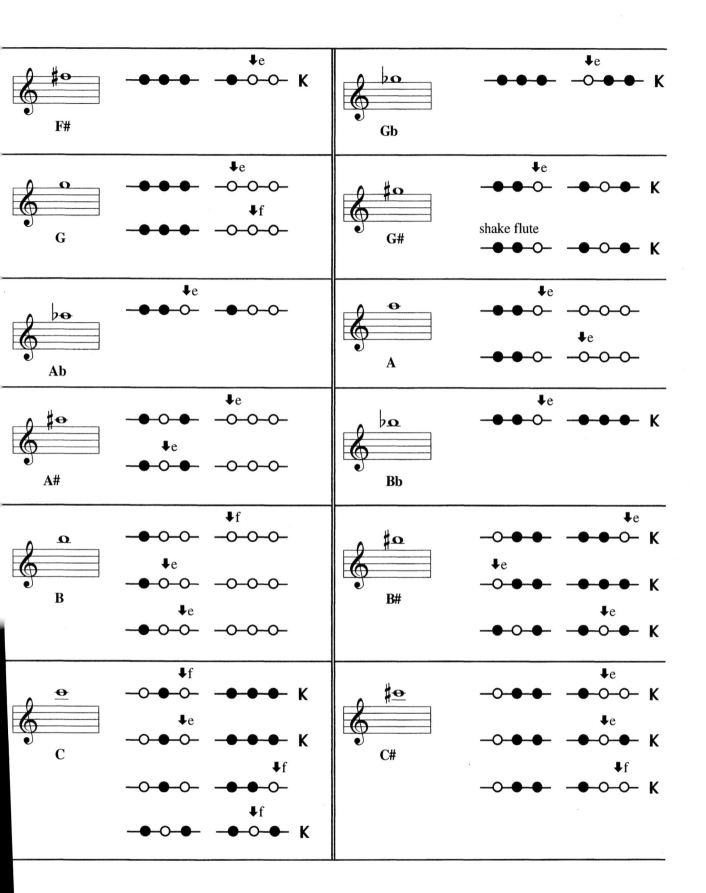

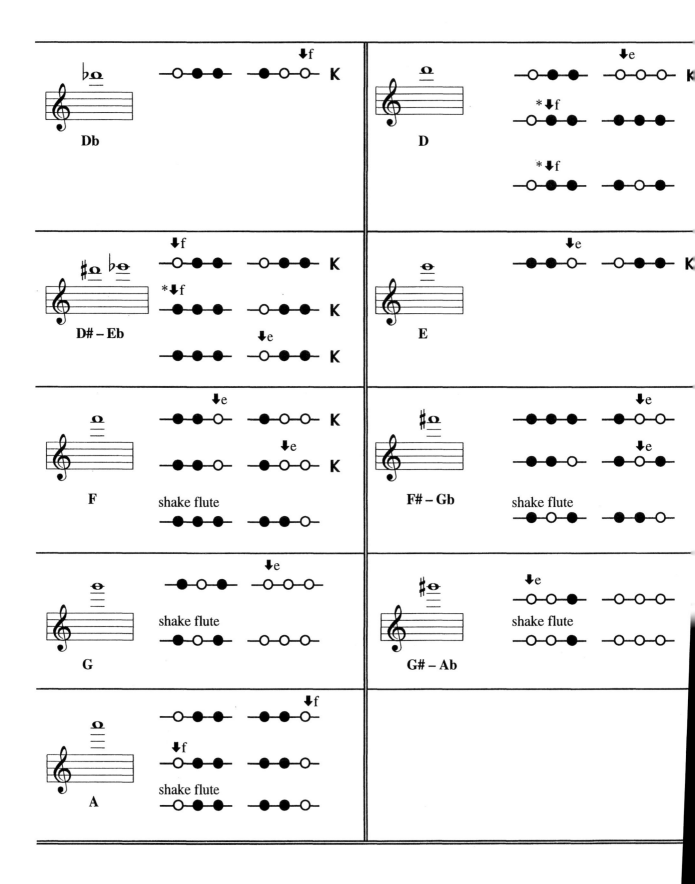

100

CHAPTER IV

EXERCISES AND TUNES TO PLAY

Illustration from Thomas Cahusac, *Cahusac's Pocket Companion for the German-Flute*. London: Cahusac, c. 1790–1802.

ABOUT THE MUSIC

The passions remain necessary to be expressed....we should endeavor to play in that manner which is most likely to affect the heart....

(Longman and Lukey, c. 1775, Vol. II, p. 3)

The exercises and tunes in this chapter are taken from flute tutors and other little books published for the flute dating 1707–1851. Remember that the one-keyed flute was still in use long after keyed flutes made their appearance in the second half of the eighteenth century.

Treatises from the eighteenth century are full of simple tunes—most are void of scale exercises and tone studies of the kind found in modern method books. The tunes and exercises that follow were chosen to give you a broad spectrum of the pieces played by eighteenth- and nineteenth-century flutists. None of the exercises or selections in this chapter were composed by twentieth-century composers, so you'll be learning the one-keyed flute by playing the same tunes as did your eighteenth-century counterparts. Many of the tunes are taken from later eighteenth-century sources so as to avoid excessive ornamentation.

The tunes are arranged by key. The simplest key, D major, is first, followed by G major, e minor, and so on. Each key is preceded by a word about the passion it implies.

Find a one-keyed flutist with whom to play duets. Your progress will be faster and more enjoyable if you play with others.

Heron (1771, p. 48) gives us a standard for which to strive as we play flute duets:

Duet Playing

> In the performance of duets,...two German flutes agreeing in tone and mode of expression, appear to great advantage;...no harsh forced sound should be suffered by any means; the contest should be, who would give the sweetest and most harmonious tone; a sound that should seem rather singing or floating in the air, than proceeding from any instrument.

D Major

D Major is by nature somewhat shrill and stubborn; it is best suited to noisy, joyful, warlike, and rousing things. But, at the same time, nobody will deny that when a flute is used instead of a trumpet, and a violin instead of kettle-drums, even this hard key can give a special disposition to delicate things.

Mattheson (1713, p. 242–243)

D major is the easiest key for the one-keyed flute. Most notes in the scale are directly fingered.

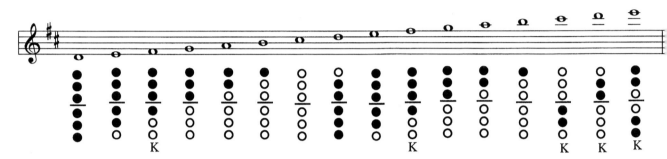

In the following exercise, Tromlitz (1791, p. 13) recommends that the player hold each note as long as the breath allows, while turning the flute first slightly outward, then inward, until you find the right spot and the tone becomes firm, full, and strong. Play slowly. Allow the fingers time to gently find the next open tone hole as you cover one tone hole at a time.

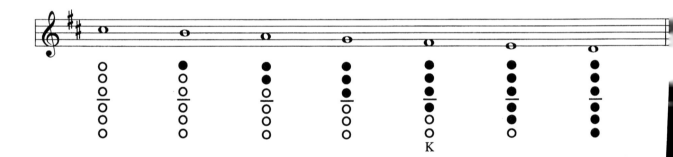

Now try this little tune. Depress the key only for f sharp.

Exercises for Proper Fingerings

When playing these exercises, be sure to open the key for f sharp and close it for e natural.

from Tulou

Interval Studies in D Major

Tune the intervals carefully. Be sure that f sharp is not flat.

after Lindsay

Intonation Check

Tune the octaves carefully.

after Dr. Arnold

after Dr. Arnold

Are you fingering e natural correctly?

after Dr. Arnold

107

Interval Studies on Low D

Tromlitz (1791, p. 132) tells us to check that the high and low notes are equally in tune, so that one octave is not sharper or flatter than the other.

after Tromlitz

Tune the difference tones carefully.

after Tulou

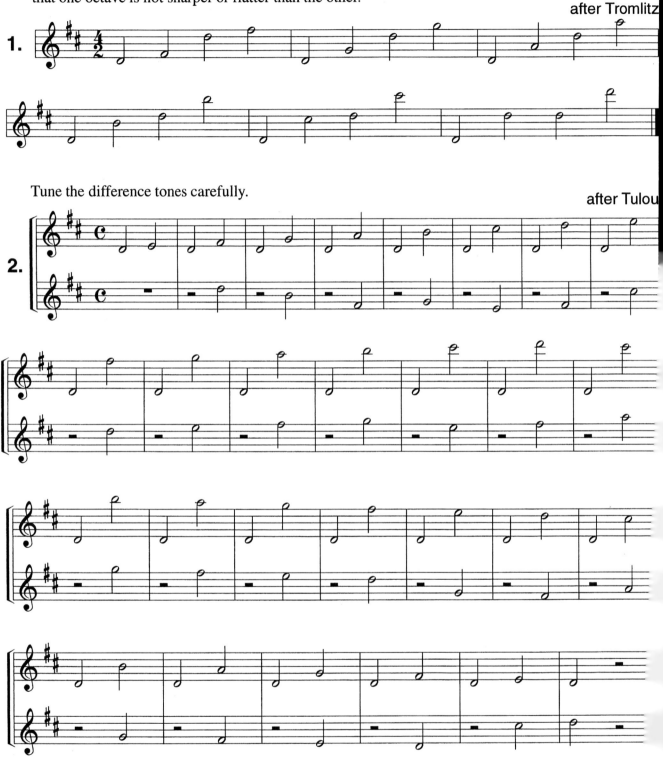

Allegretto

after Tulou

3.

109

Scale Studies In D Major

Tune the intervals carefully.

after Tulou

First Tunes
in D Major

La Belle Catherine

from Wra

Battle of Prague

from Wra

Robin Adair: Irish Air

from Crar

Aldridge's Allemand

from Longman & Lukey

1) You may keep the Key open (depressed) when moving from f-sharp to a-natural and back again.

Rigadoon

from the Modern Musick-Master

Vainly now you strive

Dr. Arne
from Dr. Arnold's Instructions

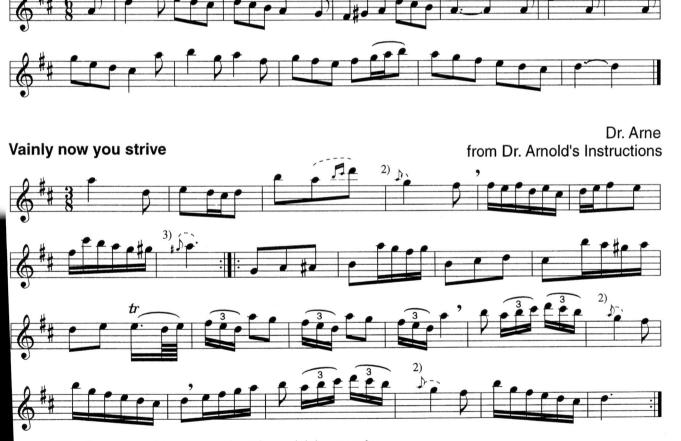

2) Give these appoggiaturas approximately an eighth-note value.
3) Give these appoggiaturas approximately a quarter-note value.

To thee Oh! gentle Sleep.

Mr. Martin
from Dr. Arnold's Instructions

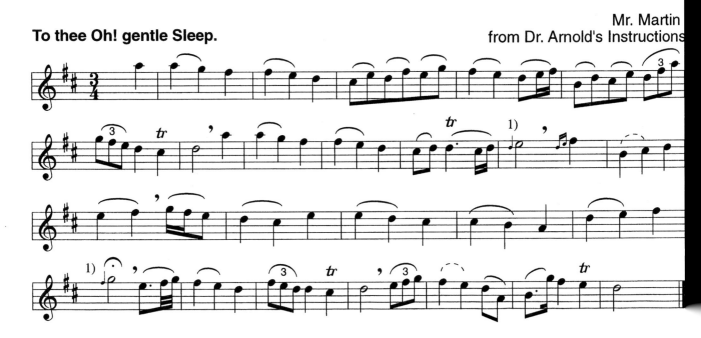

1) Give the appoggiaturas approximately a quarter-note value.

English Hornpipe

from Alexander

2) The grace notes in the Hornpipe are quick.

3) James Alexander tells us that the vertical wedge indicates the note is to be played very short and distinctly
—even shorter than a staccato note (indicated by a dot).

114

Six Minuets

from The Modern Musick-Master (1730)

The six minuets which follow are all in 3/4 time. The Modern Musick-Master states that minuets in 3/2 are slow, and those in 3/8 are very quick; those in 3/4 lie somewhere in between. Omit the ornaments at first. Concentrate instead on producing a well-centered tone and on playing in tune. Later when you add the ornaments, try those suggested in the examples below, or read Chapter III "On Trills" for further guidance.

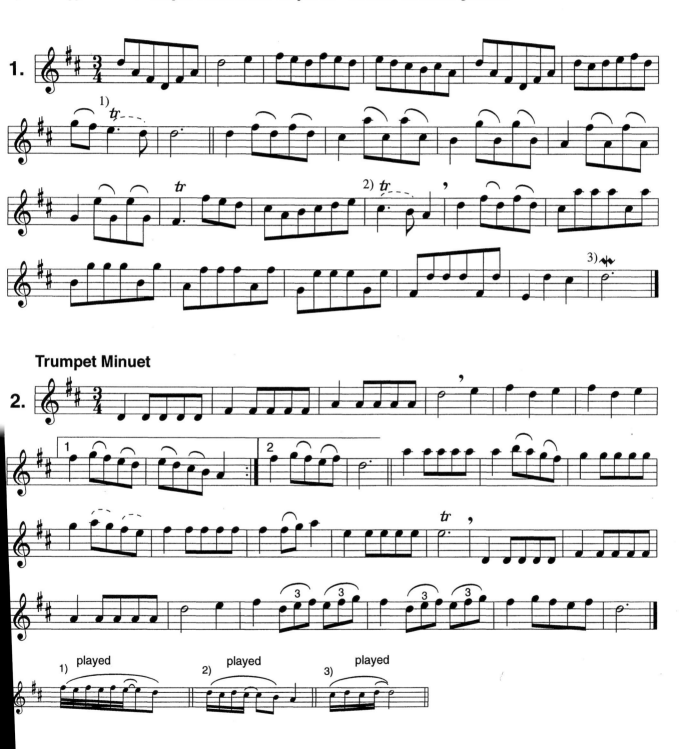

Trumpet Minuet

Fingering Reminders:

```
c''' sharp    _ _ _ / 4 5 _ K
d'''          _ 2 3 / _ _ _ K
```

Minuet

3.

Minuet

4.

played ("double jiggle")   played

3) Try a "double jiggle" here. See Chapter III, "On Trills."

Tunes In D Major
from the Delightful Pocket Companion (c. 1745)

Omit the ornaments at first. Later add just one at a time. Read Chapter III, "On Trills" for guidance.

Love's a Gentle Generous Passion

Minuet

Prussian March

But if thou

Try a 'double jiggle' here. See Chapter III, "On Trills."

119

Experiment with tongue groupings and slurs. Try "tdt" (see Chapter II, *On Articulation*), or a slur-two-tongue-one grouping for the triplet figures.

Air by M. Festing

5.

1) If your tempo is quick, consider using this fingering for c''' sharp.

 _ 2 3 / 4 _ _ K

What a Beau my Granny was

Cahusac's Pocket Companion

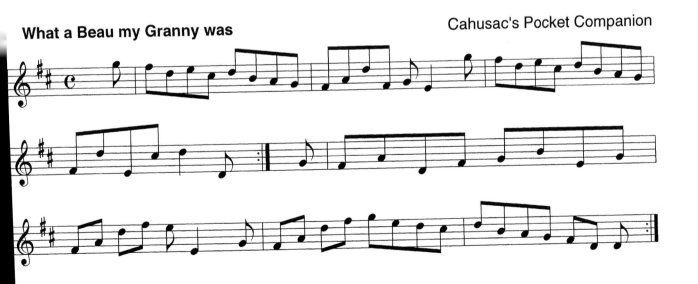

Maggie Lawder
from Longman and Lukey (c.1775)

Duets in D Major

from The Delightful Pocket Companion (c. 1745)

Minuet

1.

Fine

D.C. al Fine

Play the march lightly. Space all eighth notes.

March

2.

Duett by Mr. Hasse

Air by Mr. Weideman

Air by Mr. Weideman

Duets in D Major

from Longman & Lukey (c. 1775)

Dorsetshire March

Menuetto by Mr. Tacet

2.

128

played

Practice Hint:

Remember to omit the ornaments at first. You'll have enough to think about—tone, intonation, proper fingerings, etc.
Add the ornaments only when everything else is in place.

Duet

3.

Air by Mr. Handel

4.

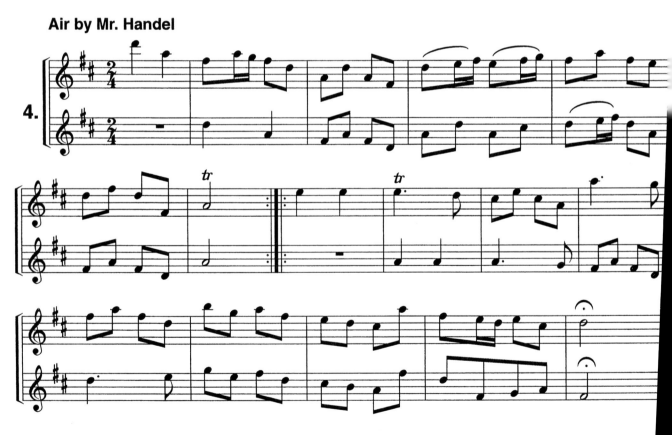

130

More Duets in D Major

Allegretto poco Andante

W.A. Mozart
from Tulou

131

Allegretto

Devienne

G Major

*G Major is a very persuasive and expressive key; it is also quite brilliant and is
suited both to serious and to cheerful things.*

Mattheson (1713, p. 243)

G major is also an easy key. Most notes in the scale are directly fingered.

133

Interval Studies in G Major

Tune the intervals carefully. Be sure that f sharp is not flat.

after Lindsay

Intonation Check

after Dr. Arnold

Tune the octaves carefully.

Scale Studies in G Major

Tune the intervals carefully.

after Tulou

First Tunes in G Major

<u>Fingering Reminders:</u>

```
f'' natural   1 2 3 / 4 _ 6
c'' natural   _ 2 3 / _ _ _
c''' natural  _ 2 _ / 4 5 6 K
```

Rigadoon

from The Modern Musick-Master

A Dialogue Between Damon and Celimena

from the Beggar's Opera

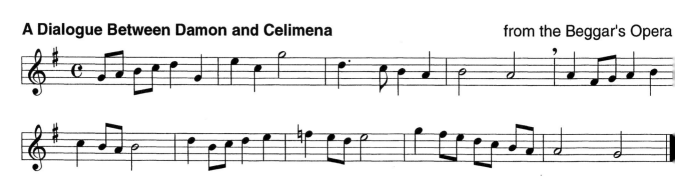

Menuet

Mussard

1) Play this grace note with approximately a quarter-note value.
2) Try playing this grace note quickly and on the beat.

Songs from the Beggar's Opera

John Gay, the creator of the highly popular 1728 Beggar's Opera, used existing tunes for the songs in the opera. The composers of the tunes, where known, are noted here.

London Ladies

Vivace

1.

All in the Downs   P. G. Sandoni

Larghetto

2.

Cease your funning

3.

139

Would Fate to me Belinda give

John Wilford

Good-morrow, Gossip Joan

Hornpipe

Tunes In G Major
from the Delightful Pocket Companion (c. 1745)

Blowzabella

TEXT: Of Anna's charms let others tell, Of bright Eliza's beauty;
My song shall be of Blowzabel, To sing of her's my duty.

Air by Mr. Pescelti

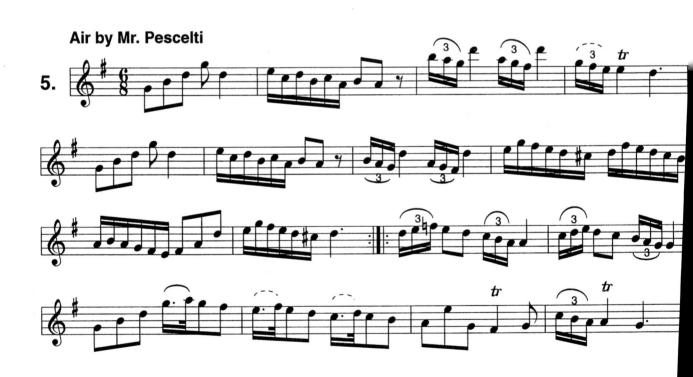

Minuet by Mr. Martini

Three Minuets in G Major
from the Modern Musick-Master (1730)

Duets in G Major

W. A. Mozart
from Tulou

Andante

Romance

Haydn
arr. Vanderhagen

1) Vanderhagen (1790, p. 36) tells us that the notes with wedges are to be played staccato.

147

148

Allegro

Devienne

149

Duets in G Major
from the Delightful Pocket Companion (c. 1745)

Minuet by Mr. Gizzietto

1.

Italian Peasants

La Confession

Blavet

151

E Minor

E minor can hardly be considered joyful, no matter what one does with it, because it is normally very pensive, profound, grieved and sad, though in such a way that there is still hope for consolation. Something quick might well be set in it, but this does not mean that the key becomes at once joyful. It loves grief and pain.

Mattheson (1713, p. 239)

E minor is also an easy key. Most notes in the scale are directly fingered.

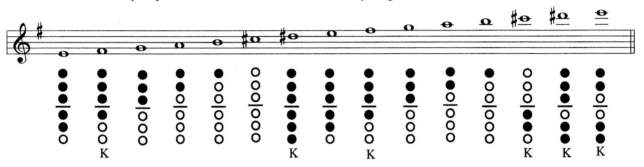

Prelude

Corrette

Prelude by octaves

Corrett

Prelude by sevenths

Corret

152

Intonation Check

Tune the octaves carefully.
Be sure you are using the proper fingerings for first
and second octave e natural: 1 2 3 / 4 5 _

after Dr. Arnold

1) Consider using this fingering for both c-sharps: _ _ _ / 4 5 _ K
2) Consider using this fingering for d''': _ 2 3 / 4 5 6 or _ 2 3 / 4 _ 6
3) Try this alternate fingering for both c' and c'': _ 2 _ / 4 5 6 K

153

Scale Studies In E Minor

Tune the intervals carefully.

after Tulou

1) Are you fingering d-sharp correctly?

155

Interval Studies in E Minor

Tune the intervals carefully. Play slowly!
Be sure that f sharp is not flat.

after Lindsay

Exercises in E Minor
by Vanderhagen (c. 1790)

Are you fingering d-sharp correctly? 1 2 3 / 4 5 6 K

Tunes in E Minor

from The Delightful Pocket Companion (c. 1745)

Minuet by Mr. Handel

1.

Minuet by Mr. Petsold

2.

Dubourg's Minuet

159

Minuet

Corrette

160

Gigue en Rondeau

Fine

D.S. al Fine

Rondeau

Michel Blave

Fine

162

D.C. al Fine

First Duet in e minor

from *First Book of Pieces*

Blavet often indicated breath marks with an "h" (for *haleine*).
The breaths marked with a comma in this duet are Blavet's.

Duets in e minor

from Vanderhagen (c. 1800)

Vanderhagen (c. 1800, p. 38) tells us to give this appoggiatura an eighth-note value.
Vanderhagen tells us to give this appoggiatura a quarter-note value.

More Duets in e minor

from Vanderhagen (c. 1800)

Pastorale

3.

1) Vanderhagen (c. 1800, p. 36) tells us that notes with wedges are to be played staccato.

Allegretto

Three Duets in e minor

from Devienne's Méthode (c. 1792)

1) Play the grace note with an eighth note value.

Grazioso

2.

Lise chantait

3.

1) Give this grace note an eighth note value.
2) Play these grace notes quickly and before the beat

A Major

A Major is very gripping, although at the same time brilliant, and is more suited to lamenting and sad passions than to divertissements.

Mattheson (1713, p. 288)

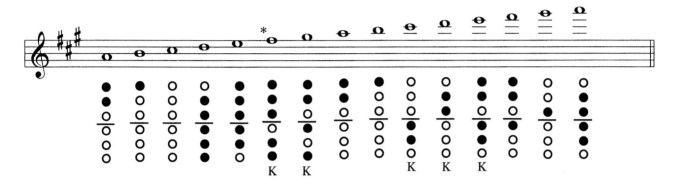

*The common fingering for f sharp (1 2 3 / 4 _ _ K) is flat in relationship to g sharp. Quantz and others recommend the use of an alternate f sharp fingering (listed above) when f sharp lies next to g sharp **in slow movements.** The alternate f sharp is a weaker note than that produced with the traditional fingering, but its higher pitch more closely matches the notes around it. It is not mandatory that you use this alternate fingering, but give it a try. In quick passages, however, feel free to use the regular f sharp fingering. Read the section titled "Alternate f sharp" in Chapter Three, *Fingerings for the One-Keyed Flute,* for further discussion regarding this alternate f sharp fingering.

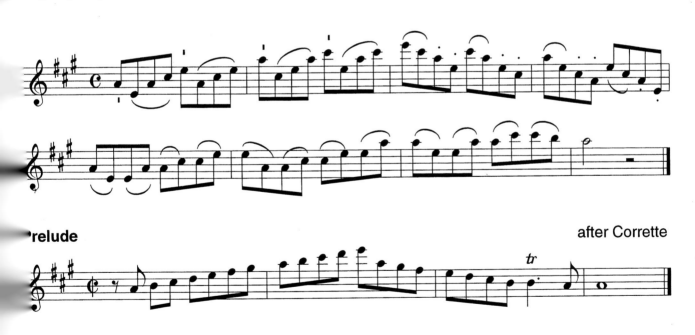

Prelude

after Corrette

Prelude   after Corrette

Prelude   Corrette

1) Don't guess at the trill fingerings! Look them up and write them down for future reference.

Intonation Check

after Dr. Arnold

Tune the octaves carefully.

2) At quick tempos, try this alternate fingering for d'''   _ 2 3 / 4 _ 6

Interval Studies in A Major

Tune the intervals carefully.
Be especially attentive to g sharp, which is quite sharp in the first and second octaves.

after Lindsay

Scale Studies in A Major

Beginner players should feel free abbreviate these studies by omitting those notes above e'''.
Tune the intervals carefully.

after Tulou

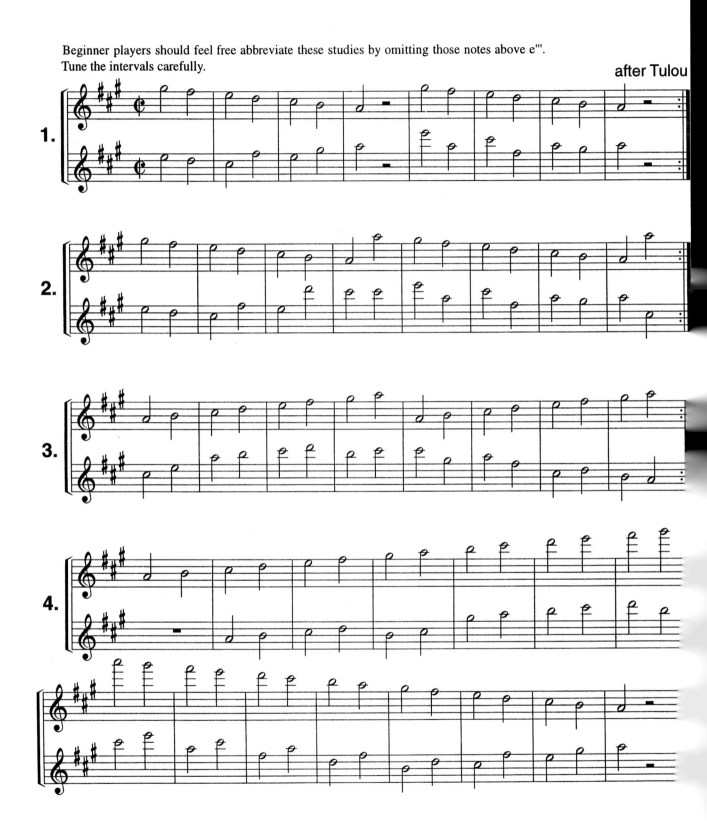

174

Tunes in A Major

Minuet

Modern Musick-Master

Vanderhagen

Would Fate to me Belinda give

Musical Miscellany

176

First Tambourine

Delightful Pocket Companion

Second Tambourine

Fine

D.C. al Fine

) f" natural is fingered 1 2 3 / 4 _ 6

177

Tunes from Cahusac's
Pocket Companion (c. 1780)

Cortillion. The Sprig of Myrtle.

Allemand

Allemand

3.

Fine

D.C. al Fine

179

Eccho Minuet
from The Modern Musick-Master (1730)

* This trill fingering is not what you'd expect. Look it up!

Two Duets in A Major

from Devienne's Methode (c 1792)

CHAPTER V

MODERN STUDIES FOR THE ONE-KEYED FLUTE

Illustration from Jean-Louis Tulou, *Méthode de Flûte.*
Mainz: Schott, 1853.

INTRODUCTION TO
MODERN STUDIES

---

*...[there is] a mistaken idea, that there is no other method of proceeding, than by practicing what are called easy or common tunes; in which several years may be spent, without the learner's being, in reality, so far advanced in his progress, as one that had been only **one week** practicing his scale of D, in a rational and systematic manner.*

Gunn (c. 1793, p. 23)

There is a real temptation on the part of today's one-keyed flutist to skip the systematic building of technique and proceed directly to the solo repertoire. Don't be one of those players. As is true with modern flute playing, technique is built through the practicing of tone studies, scales, thirds, chords, etc.

The following are modern exercises which I designed for the one-keyed flute. Not all keys are covered; the exercises are limited to 4 sharps and 3 flats. You will rarely find literature which extends beyond these boundaries.

Play the following exercises *slowly*. Pay extraordinary attention to use of proper fingerings. Keep that fingering chart handy!

Establish a systematic practice routine for yourself that includes all the building blocks you need. Some ideas are listed below.

Practice Routine

1) Tone Studies: Play the first pages of one of the key centers in this book (for example, pages 104–111 of the D Major section).

2) Scales, thirds, chords: Play the exercises that follow. Also see Appendix B for books of Studies for the one-keyed flute. You'll enjoy working on Quantz's *Solfeggi*, for example. If you have access to Müller, *Elementarbuch* (c. 1815), you'll find forty-six pages of exercises in many keys.

3) Simple tunes : —such as those found in this book.

4) Duet playing: Easy duets are to be found in this book. If you don't have a duet partner, play duets with yourself. Tape record yourself playing one part, then play the other part as you play back the recording.

5) Solo repertoire : See Appendix A for repertoire suggestions.

Major Sequences for the One-Keyed Flute

in the most common keys

Beginning players: begin with the exercises in D, G, and C Major.

by Jan Bola

* Consider using alternate f sharp when it lies next to g sharp.
Alternate f' sharp: 1 2 3 / _ 5 6
Alternate f'' sharp: 1 2 3 / _ 5 6 K

* FINGERING REMINDER:
b" flat   1 2 _ / 4 5 6 K

* FINGERING REMINDER:
e" flat   1 2 3 / 4 5 6 K

Broken Chord Studies

in the major keys

u may omit the highest notes found in brackets.

by Jan Boland

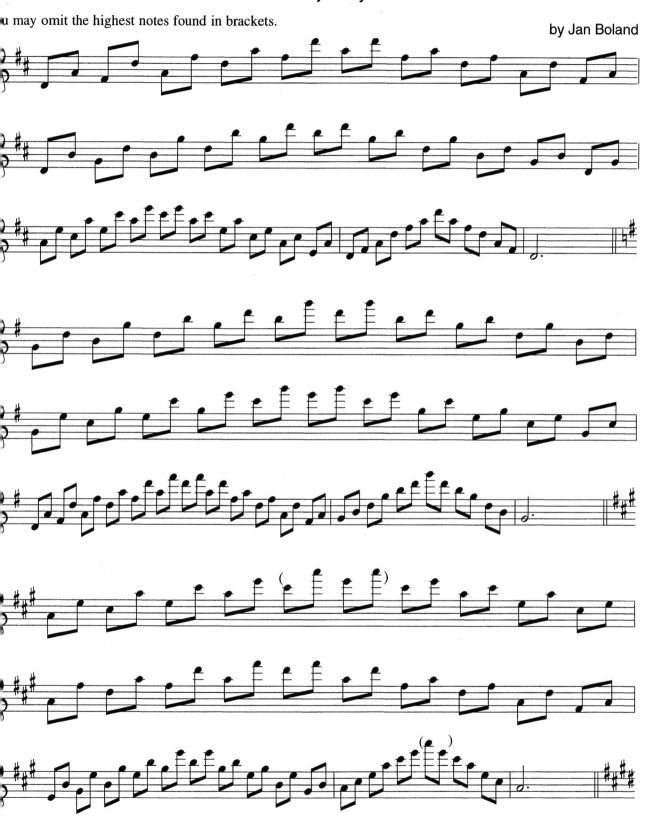

189

190

Broken Chord Studies
in the minor keys

You may omit the highest notes found in brackets.

APPENDIX A

THE "TOP 13" EIGHTEENTH-CENTURY FLUTE TUTORS

The following thirteen tutors were selected from among nearly two hundred I surveyed and represent our best resources for learning to play the one-keyed flute. The tutors span the years from 1707 to 1793, the period between the publication of Hotteterre's *Principes*, the first tutor written for the one-keyed flute, and the time when the popularity of the one-keyed flute began to fade.

The tutors are listed in chronological order. A general overview of each tutor is given, and the existence of facsimile editions (unchanged reprints) and modern translations is identified.

Jacques Hotteterre (le Romain)
Principes de la flûte traversière, ou flûte d'Allemagne. . .
[Principles of the transverse or German flute. . .]
Paris: Christophe Ballard, 1707. 50p

Hotteterre's *Principes* (1707) was the first tutor for the one-keyed flute to appear in any country. It is our primary source of information for the flute and its performance practices in the late seventeenth and early eighteenth century. We can assume that this tutor was very popular from its numerous subsequent editions and translations, which also enabled it to become the most influential tutor published before Quantz's *Versuch* (1752). The author, Jacques Hotteterre (1674–1763), was a French flutist, composer, and teacher at the courts of Louis XIV and Louis XV. He was born into an esteemed family of musical instrument makers. His *Principes* has three parts; the first, a tutor for the one-keyed flute, is followed by short tutors for the recorder and oboe.

The special strengths of this tutor are its discussions of intonation, articulation, rhythmic inequality (the uneven performance of quick notes, or *notes inégales*), and ornaments. Because the one-keyed flute has special intonation problems, Hotteterre gives the reader specific embouchure adjustments to make for each note and trill to correct the intonation. He discusses the articulation syllables used by flutists in early eighteenth-century France (*tu* and *ru*) and includes musical examples so that the reader can study their practical application. He describes various French ornaments (*tremblement, battement, flattement, accent, port de voix,* and *coulement)* in the chapter on ornamentation, illustrating their usage with musical examples; the *flattement* is a fingered vibrato.

Two facsimile editions of Hotteterre's tutor are currently available:

1. Kassel: Bärenreiter, 1942. From the edition by Roger, Amsterdam, c. 1710. Also includes a modern German translation by Hans Joachim Hellwig.

2. Geneva: Minkoff Reprint, 1973. From the edition by Ballard, Paris, 1720. [Published with a facsimile of Delusse, *L'art de la flûte traversière* (Paris, c. 1760)].

An English translation of the c. 1710 Roger edition by Paul Marshall Douglas is published as *Principles of the Flute, Recorder and Oboe* (New York: Dover, 1983). With introduction and notes. An English translation of the 1707 edition by David Lasocki, *Principles of the Flute, Recorder and Oboe* (New York: Praeger, 1968), is currently out of print.

[Peter Prelleur]

The Modern Musick-Master or the Universal Musician...

London: Printing-Office in Bow Church-Yard, 1730. 48p

The Modern Musick-Master, compiled by Peter Prelleur, is a collection of six tutors for various instruments. The third tutor in the collection, for one-keyed flute, is titled *The Newest Method for Learners on the German Flute.*

The Newest Method is representative of numerous anonymous tutors which appeared in England in the eighteenth century. It is essentially an edited, abridged edition of an English translation of Hotteterre's *Principes* which appeared c. 1729. Actually, Hottetere's tutor and its subsequent editions were the primary instructional books for the flute available in the English language prior to about 1770 when a tutor by Lewis Granom (*Instructions*) appeared. *The Newest Method* was perhaps the most popular of all anonymous flute tutors and strongly influenced flute playing in England during the early part of the eighteenth century.

The only chapter not drawn from Hotteterre's *Principes* is the chapter on meter which contains information on the relative tempi of various duple and triple meter signs. This material is based on information in Hotteterre's *L'art de preluder* (1719) and on Freillon-Poncein's *La veritable maniere,* 1700.

Thirty-three charming tunes for the flute (not found in Hotteterre's *Principes)* are included. Some are short dance movements, and some are more lengthy airs from operas of the day.

Two facsimile editions of Prelleur's tutor are currently available:

1. Kassel: Bärenreiter, 1965. Edited by Alexander Hyatt King. An unchanged reprint of the complete *Modern Musick-Master.*

2. London: Bärenreiter Ltd., 1965. Edited by Alexander Hyatt King. An unchanged reprint of only *The Newest Method for Learners on the German Flute,* the portion dealing with the one-keyed flute.

Michel Corrette

Méthode pour apprendre aisément à jouer de la flûte traversière

[Method for learning to play the transverse flute easily]

Paris: Boivin & Le Clerc, c. 1734. 50p

Corrette (1709–1795) earned his living by playing the organ and composing for amateur musicians of the rising middle class. Corrette's *Méthode,* also written for the amateur, includes instruction on the basic principles of music, chapters on preluding and transposition, and a few simple airs and duets. It is a good source of information about French performance practices of the second quarter of the eighteenth century. Corrette's is the first method for the four-piece flute, and is the first to mention the piccolo. Corrette lists piccolo concertos with which he is familiar. The tutor is valuable for its treatment of meter, ornamentation, articulation, and preluding.

Corrette compares and contrasts the use of meter in French, Italian, English, and German music, and the performance of *notes inégales* is explained within the context of each meter.

Corrette supports Hotteterre's definitions of various musical ornaments and provides musical examples. He also tells the reader which ornaments are appropriate to improvise when none are indicated in the music. He treats the *flattement,* a vibrato-like effect produced with the finger, as an ornament and indicates when to use it by marking specific notes in sample solo airs and duets. Corrette dismisses the *tu* and *ru* articulation syllables of Hotteterre as old-fashioned, recommending instead a simple tongue attack. Finally, he includes examples of easy preludes with instructions on how to improvise them.

Four facsimile editions are currently available:

1. Hildesheim: George Olms, 1975.

2. Buren: Frits Knuf, 1978. Introduction and notes by Mirjam Nastasi.

3. Geneva: Minkoff Reprint, 1977. From the *nouvelle édition*, Paris, c. 1773.

4. Firenze: Studio per Edizioni Scelte, 1995.

An English translation by Carol Reglin Farrar is published as *Michel Corrette and Flute-Playing in the Eighteenth Century* (Brooklyn, New York: Institute of Mediaeval Music, 1970). Includes some errors in the text and musical examples.

Johann Joachim Quantz

Versuch einer Anweisung die Flöte traversiere zu spielen

[Essay of a method for playing the transverse flute]

Berlin: Johann Friedrich Voss, 1752. 334p

Quantz's *Versuch* is a monumental tutor that reflects the musical practices of the period c. 1725-1755 in Dresden and Berlin. J. J. Quantz (1697-1773) worked first at the Dresden Court, then became the flute teacher of Frederick the Great of Prussia.

The influence of Quantz's *Versuch* was both immediate and lasting. It has been the subject of many reprints, translations, and "borrowings" for over two hundred years. The book was published simultaneously in French and German, and a Dutch translation appeared within two years. Edward R. Reilly's modern English translation and studies are exemplary.

Versuch was not written as a do-it-yourself manual for the amateur flutist, as were the earlier tutors, but as a treatise containing the clear and insightful observations of a celebrated professional performer and teacher. The tutor is in three parts, only the first of which is dedicated exclusively to flute instruction. The second part addresses the art of accompanying and matters of good ensemble playing, and the third part discusses musical form and style.

Perhaps the greatest strengths of *Versuch* for the flute player are Quantz's discussions of the embouchure, ornamentation, and articulation. The *Versuch* is the only tutor prior to Gunn's *Art* (c. 1793) to offer any more than the simplest description of the flexibility required of the embouchure in producing octaves and dynamics. Quantz devotes several chapters to ornamentation, dividing it into two categories—essential ornaments (generally indicated in the music by means of signs) and arbitrary ornaments (often left to the taste of the player). Of particular note is his chapter "Of the Manner of Playing the Adagio," which includes an Adagio movement notated first as a simple melody, then ornamented. The chapter devoted to articulation is full of musical examples that illustrate the articulation syllables (*ti, di, tiri, diri, did'll*) practiced at this time in Germany. Quantz's is the first tutor to show double- tonguing syllables. Three facsimile editions are currently available:

1. Wiesbaden: Breitkopf & Härtel, 1988. From the 1st edition, Berlin, 1752. Introduction in German and English by Barthold Kuijken.

2. Kassel: Bärenreiter, 1953. From the 3rd edition, Berlin, 1789. With notes in German by Hans-Peter Schmitz. New version with notes by Horst Augsbach, 1983.

3. *Essai d'une méthode pour apprendre à joüer de la flûte traversière*. Paris: Zurfluh, 1975. From the French edition, Berlin, 1752. Introduction in French by Pierre Sechet.

An English translation by Edward R. Reilly is published as *On Playing the Flute*, 2nd ed. (New York: Schirmer Books, 1985). With introduction and notes.

Antoine Mahaut

Nieuwe Manier om binnen korten tyd op de Dwarsfluit te leeren speelen. / Nouvelle Méthode pour apprendre en peu de tems à joüer de la flûte traversière

[A new method for learning to play the transverse flute in a short time]

Second edition. Amsterdam: J. J. Hummel, 1759. 36p

Nieuwe Manier was written at a time when the one-keyed flute was at the height of its popularity. Mahaut (c. 1720–c. 1785) was a distinguished Dutch flutist and composer, today chiefly remembered for his tutor. He stated in his introduction that the purpose of his book was to expand Hotteterre's excellent *Principes* and thereby fulfill current pedagogical needs. The text of the second edition (listed above) was written in French and Dutch in parallel columns.

Mahaut's tutor was to be used by both beginners and more advanced players. It is wonderfully clear and concise. Of all the eighteenth-century tutors, this one is probably the best to work with for learning to play the one-keyed flute. Its special strengths include the chapters on intonation, articulation, ornamentation, and alternate fingerings. Directions are given for correcting faulty intonation by adjusting the embouchure, using alternate fingerings, and changing the middle joints or moving the cork.

Mahaut's chapter on flute articulation confirms that the syllables of Hotteterre (*tu* and *ru*) were being abandoned in favor of patterns featuring slurred and detached notes—patterns he illustrates in a two-page Allegro. In addition, Mahaut recommends using the syllables *di-del* for the new double-tongue articulation.

Mahaut identifies the differences between the Italian and French performance styles of specific ornaments, illustrating them with musical examples. An entire chapter is devoted to those alternate fingerings to be used to correct intonation and provide greater ease of execution.

On the light side, the tutor mentions two peculiar techniques—holding the flute to the left instead of the right, and placing the flute between the upper lip and the nose and blowing it from underneath! Mahaut did not recommend either.

One facsimile is currently available:

Geneva: Minkoff Reprint, 1972. French text. (Paris: La Chevardière, 1759)

An English translation by Eileen Hadidian is published as *A New Method for Learning to Play the Transverse Flute* (Bloomington: Indiana University Press, 1989). An earlier translation by Pauline E. Durichen, "New Method for the Transverse Flute," appeared in *Divisions*, Vol. 1 no. 1 (September 1978): 20–34; Vol. 1 no. 2 (December 1978): 28–46.

[Charles] Delusse

L'art de la flûte traversière

[The art of the transverse flute]

Paris: the author, c. 1760. 49p

Delusse (c. 1720–1774), was a Parisian flutist and composer. His flute tutor *L'art,* which is drawn, in part, from a violin tutor titled *The Art of Playing on the Violin* by Geminiani (London, 1751), also presents unique ideas about flute technique, including a curious way to produce vibrato and an introduction to the double tongue.

The special strengths of this tutor lie in its discussion of articulation, vibrato, harmonics, and in its music. *L'art* is the first French flute tutor to mention the double tongue. Delusse recommends the syllable *loul* be used for the double tongue, gives a sign that designates its use in the printed score, and provides a Vivace movement in which he indicates when it is to be used. The articulation *hu* is to be used in slow, tender movements.

Delusse describes three methods of producing vibrato. The first is a curious method that requires the player to roll the body of the flute in and out by manipulating the left thumb. The second method is a type of breath vibrato produced by activating the lungs and puffing the syllables *hou, hou*; this is the first tutor in the eighteenth century to mention breath vibrato. The third method, *flattement,* is to be used only on long notes.

L'art is the first French flute tutor to mention harmonics and explain how they are structured, notated, and produced. Delusse provides a Largo movement using numerous sequences of harmonics. It is also the first French tutor to assign specific passions to the manner in which ornaments are executed. The tutor is full of interesting music. First we find preludes in twenty keys. Next we see very early examples of progressive lessons for the flute; previous eighteenth-century tutors customarily introduced only a few easy musical studies to accompany the text. Finally, and perhaps most curiously, the tutor contains twelve long and very difficult caprices, also called cadenzas According to Bowers (1971, p. 330), these caprices are unprecedented in difficulty and style, and mark the beginnings of the flute etude in France. Three facsimile editions are currently available:

1. Geneva: Minkoff Reprints, 1973. From the Paris c. 1759 edition containing only one page of text. [Published with Hotteterre, *Principes de la flûte traversière* (Paris, 1707).]

2. Columbus, Ohio: Early Music Facsimiles. From the Paris, c. 1760 edition.

3. Buren: Frits Knuf, 1980. From the Paris c. 1760 edition. With introduction and notes in English by Greta Moens-Haenen.

Lewis Granom
Plain and Easy Instructions for Playing on the German-Flute
The Third Edition with Additions
London: T. Bennett, c. 1770. 174p

Granom (c. 1725–c. 1791) was a flutist and trumpeter from London. His *Instructions* represent the first effort by an Englishman to provide the amateur flutist with a more scholarly flute tutor than was currently available in the popular little English books of instruction by anonymous authors.

While some of Granom's instructions are borrowed directly from earlier sources, he presents original ideas concerning tone production (suggesting that the player "retain" the breath), gives a detailed account of double- and triple-tonguing practices, and does not hesitate to express his dislike for the newly-developed keyed flute. In fact, Granom's is the first tutor by a named author to make reference to the keyed flute. He does not approve of the additional keys, saying that they encumber the instrument and, contrary to popular belief, do not enable the flute to play better in tune than the one-keyed flute.

The text is variably cynical and humorous as the author expresses strong personal opinions on several musical subjects and subsequently provides us with some entertaining reading. For example, Granom cautions the flutist not to ask a music seller for advice on what music to buy, for he may "load you with all the trash he himself has published."

Perhaps the greatest strength of this tutor is its eighteen-page trill chart; it is the most detailed trill chart for the one-keyed flute to appear anywhere. Each trill is shown with the appropriate fingerings for the preparatory note, principal note, and two closing notes.

Granom provides extensive instruction on the double-tongue (*toot-tle*), an indication of its growing importance, especially in England, during the second half of the eighteenth century. He gives us the first instruction on the triple-tongue found in any flute tutor, saying the syllables *toot-tle-too* are to be used for notes grouped in threes, and must be used in all gigues. His instruction on the double and triple tongue was plagiarized in many anonymous English tutors which followed.

Granom's is the first flute tutor to attempt to clearly define the lengths of appoggiaturas, by giving the greater appoggiatura and the lesser appoggiatura specific duration values. He says that there is no ornament "so universally approved of and so frequently used" as the appoggiatura.

Copies are listed in the holdings of these modern libraries: the Library of Congress in Washington, D.C. and the British Library in London.

Luke Heron

A Treatise on the German Flute

London: W. Griffin, 1771. 78p

Heron's *Treatise* marks the first major contribution to one-keyed flute instruction by an Englishman. The tutor is lengthy, scholarly, and complete. Heron's presentation is flowery and wordy, yet instructive.

The recurring emphasis of the text is on how to play the flute musically and sensitively in response to the passions of the music. The musical passions are a subject dwelt upon frequently by German writers, but rarely by an Englishman.

The special strengths of the tutor are the chapters on breathing, intonation, ornamentation, and articulation. Heron's *Treatise* is one of the earliest tutors to address the subject of the breath, saying no force is necessary. Heron cautions the reader against the aspirated breath *hogh*, indicating that it is a common error.

Heron emphatically declares that the flute can be played in tune despite many comments by his contemporaries to the contrary. He devotes much discussion to intonation, demanding that the player listen, and suggests specific embouchure changes to adjust pitch. Heron further recommends using a shorter middle joint during the first five minutes of playing to accommodate the instrument's flat pitch when cold.

The Heron tutor reflects changes in ornamentation practices that took place as the eighteenth century progressed. While earlier tutors discussed many and varied ornaments, the only ornaments referred to by Heron are the trill and the long appoggiatura (one which receives half the value of the principal note).

The articulation syllables so common in the early part of the century are not mentioned here. Instead, Heron recommends the use of the syllable *tit* (with clear instructions on where to place the tongue) for most tones and stresses the importance of incorporating a good double tongue (*tit-tle*) into one's playing. He further cautions the player against too much slurring, recommending instead an alteration of slurred and tongued notes.

To my knowledge, the only extant copy of this tutor is in the Library of Congress in Washington, D.C.

Antonio Lorenzoni

Saggio per ben sonare il flauto traverso

[Essay for playing the transverse flute well]

Vicenza: Francesco Modena, 1779. 91p

Lorenzoni's *Saggio* is the only Italian tutor of significance for the one-keyed flute to appear in the eighteenth century. About one-third of the material in Lorenzoni's tutor is taken from of Quantz's *Versuch*. The remainder is original material or material borrowed from still other writers (Jean D'Alembert, Jean Rousseau, and Giuseppe Tartini). Despite this borrowing of material, we might assume that *Saggio* reflects the musical tastes of late eighteenth-century Italy.

Among the strengths of the tutor is the chapter on articulation. The complex articulation syllables described by Quantz are not reflected in Lorenzoni's tutor. Instead, Lorenzoni prescribes the use of three articulation syllables (*ti, di, ri*) in simple patterns. He also shows the use of the aspirated attack (*hi*) on repeated notes and in syncopated rhythms. Also of value is instruction on the performance practices of various musical movements (Rigadon, Preludio, etc.).

One modern facsimile edition is currently available:

Bologna, Italy: Forni, n.d. With introduction in Italian by F. Alberto Gallo.

Amand Vanderhagen

Méhode nouvelle et raisonnée pour la flûte

[New and rational method for the flute]

Paris: Boyer, c. 1790. 54p

Vanderhagen (1753–1822) was a Dutch clarinetist who moved to Paris by his early 30s. He wrote three instructional works for the flute, the first of which, *Méthode nouvelle,* is an important source on French performance practices of the Classical period. Especially notable are the chapters that reflect the changes in articulation practices that had taken place since the publication of Delusse's *L'art* (c. 1760): all articulation syllables are replaced by tongued and slurred patterns. Vanderhagen helpfully tells the reader which patterns are appropriate when the composer has not indicated any in the score.

The special features of the Vanderhagen text include his attention to tone development, performance of the *messa di voce*, and rhythmic hierarchy. Throughout the text, he stresses the importance of playing with a beautiful tone, which can be achieved through practicing slow movements and long tones. Vanderhagen also thoroughly addresses the subject of the *messa di voce* (swell), providing both written explanation and musical exercises so that the reader can learn to execute it on the flute. On the subject of rhythmic hierarchy, he discusses the strong and weak beats, so that the reader can learn which notes are to be played with more weight.

One extant copy is in the New York Public Library. No modern facsimile edition is currently available:

Johann George Tromlitz

Ausführlicher und gründlicher Unterricht die Flöte zu spielen

[Detailed and thorough instruction on playing the flute]

Leipzig: Adam Friedrich Böhme, 1791. 376p

Tromlitz's *Unterricht* stands as a giant among eighteenth-century flute tutors, probably second in importance only to Quantz's *Versuch*. The author (1725–1805) had a background in theory, composition, flute construction, and performance that is reflected in the broad coverage of the text.

The tutor was written primarily for the one-keyed flute but mentions the use of additional keys, which Tromlitz says improves the flute's tone and intonation. It therefore paves the way for the keyed flute and virtuoso playing of the nineteenth century. The special strengths of the Tromlitz tutor include its chapters on articulation, ornamentation and tone.

Although, according to Corrette, articulation syllables were already considered old-fashioned in France around 1739, they were still used in Germany at the end of the century. Tromlitz's account of tonguing and slurring practices constitutes the most comprehensive discussion of articulation in any eighteenth-century tutor. An Allegretto movement, articulated in three ways, illustrates Tromlitz's rules for applying articulation syllables to various combinations of slurred and tongued notes.

Tromlitz devotes fifty-seven pages of his tutor to ornamentation. Like Quantz, he divides ornamentation into two categories—essential ornaments and arbitrary ornaments. An Adagio movement ornamented in three ways serves as an example.

Tromlitz advocates using a more flexible embouchure than that described by previous tutors. He also recommends a tone that is even in color throughout the range of the flute—a tonal concept that anticipates that of the nineteenth century. One facsimile edition is currently available:

Buren: Frits Knuf, 1985. With introduction in English by Frans Vester.

An excellent English translation by Ardal Powell is published as *The Virtuoso Flute-Player* (Cambridge & New York: Cambridge University Press, 1991). With introduction by Eileen Hadidian.

A complete English translation can also be found in Linda Bishop Hartig, "Johann George Tromlitz's *Unterricht die Flöte zu spielen:* A Translation and Comparative Study" (Ph.D. dissertation, Michigan State University, 1981). A translation of Chapters VIII–XV only appears in Eileen Hadidian, "Johann Georg Tromlitz's Flute Treatise: Evidences of Late Eighteenth Century Performance Practice" (D.M.A. thesis, Stanford University, 1979); available from University Microfilms International, 300 N. Zeeb Road, Ann Arbor, MI 48106 ([800] 521-3042).

François Devienne
Nouvelle méthode théorique et pratique pour la flûte
[New theoretical and practical method for the flute]
Paris: Imbault, c. 1792. 77p

When the Paris Conservatory of Music was founded in 1795, Devienne (1759-1803) was appointed to its original staff of five flute professors. His flute method was immensely popular in the late eighteenth and nineteenth centuries and even survived up to 1950 in heavily modified form. It is the last significant French method for the one-keyed flute. Devienne approved of some of the extra keys but did not use them himself.

The chapters on articulation and ornamentation make this tutor an excellent source for the study of French performance practices of the Classical period. Devienne's examples of slurring practices are similar to those found in Vanderhagen's *Méthode* published two years earlier, and like Vanderhagen he also suggests appropriate articulations to use when none are indicated in the musical score. He disapproves of the practice of double tonguing, saying that it is unnatural and inhibits nuances of articulation.

Trills, turns, and appoggiaturas are the only ornaments discussed in the chapters on ornamentation, reflecting the decline from the wide variety of ornaments that existed in France early in the century.

One facsimile edition is currently available:

Florence: Studio per Edizioni Scelte, 1984. [Published in a collection titled *Tre Metodi per Flauto del Neoclassicismo Francese,* with facsimiles of Vanderhagen, *Nouvelle méthode* (q.v.), and Cambini, *Méthode pour la flûte.*]

An English translation by William Montgomery appears in his Ph.D. dissertation, "The Life and Works of François Devienne, 1759–1803" (Catholic University of America, 1975). Lacking musical examples and duets. Available from University Microfilms International.

The duets are available from Southern Music Company (San Antonio, Texas, 1967) and other publishers.

John Gunn

The Art of Playing the German-Flute on New Principles

London: the author, c. 1793. 85p

John Gunn (c. 1765–c. 1824), a Scottish flutist and a teacher of both flute and cello, lived and worked in London. *The Art of Playing the German-Flute* was the most comprehensive flute tutor to appear in England in the eighteenth century and among the most important to appear in Europe in that century as well. Because of its timely appearance and responsible treatment of flute playing, I consider it an invaluable transitional tutor from the eighteenth century to the nineteenth century.

In the opening chapter, Gunn speaks scientifically on the properties of musical sound—an approach to the subject which is unique among eighteenth-century flute tutors. Gunn also offers a reasoned and scientific approach to tone production. The result is a more detailed account than is found in other eighteenth-century tutors. Gunn's tutor reflects the conflict that existed between the emerging English concept of the large, brilliant tone as produced by the multi-keyed flute and the older ideal of a colorful, mellow tone as produced by the one-keyed flute. He approved of both kinds of tone, recommending a sound that was sometimes full and sometimes tender, thus providing variety in one's playing.

The Art does not deal with ornamentation and articulation as much as previous tutors did, but the information Gunn provides does reflect the Classical performance practices of the time. We learn that articulation practices were simple compared to those of the early eighteenth century: Gunn recommends the use of a simple *t* or *d* for general use and he introduces new syllables for double tonguing (*teddy* or *tiddy*).

In an interesting discussion of expressive playing, Gunn draws a unique and helpful analogy between oratorical expression and musical expression, and he goes on to discuss the natural rhythms inherent in musical phrases.

One facsimile edition is currently available:

Marion, Iowa: Janice Dockendorff Boland, 1992. With introduction by Janice Dockendorff Boland.

TUTORS LISTED BY NATIONALITY

FRENCH	ENGLISH	GERMAN	DUTCH	ITALIAN
Hotteterre *Principes* (1707)				
	Prelleur *Modern Musick-Master* (1730) (a translation of Hotteterre)			
Corrette *Méthode* (c. 1734)				
		Quantz *Versuch* (1752)		
			Mahaut *Nieuwe Manier* (1759)	
Delusse *L'art* (c. 1760)				
	Granom *Instructions* (c. 1770)			
	Heron *Treatise* (1771)			
				Lorenzoni *Saggio* (1779)
Vanderhagen *Méthode* (c. 1790)				
		Tromlitz *Unterricht* (1791)		
Devienne *Nouvelle méthode* (c. 1792)				
	Gunn *The Art* (c. 1793)			

APPENDIX B

ON REPERTOIRE
FOR THE BEGINNING ONE-KEYED FLUTIST

...I must give one necessary caution, which is, not to apply to a Music-Seller for his opinion in the choice of your music, especially if he publishes on his own account; for instead of recommending the works of approved authors, he immediately loads you with all the trash he himself has published....

Granom (c. 1770, p. 18–19)

Listed below are easy solos and duets for the one-keyed flute. Begin with those works in one or two sharps whose ranges do not go above e'''. You may find the German and Italian works on this list a bit easier than the French works, largely because the early French works are more highly ornamented.

Resist the temptation to attack the major repertoire as a beginning one-keyed flutist. Please save the J. S. Bach *Sonatas* for a later time when you can play well in tune, have mastered the difficult keys, and have an understanding of appropriate performance practices.

Often both a modern edition and a facsimile edition are listed. Where available, I strongly recommend that the player locate a facsimile (unedited) edition of the selected work and compare it to the modern (often-times edited) edition. Think of facsimile editions simply as photocopies of the original manuscript. With a facsimile edition in hand, you will have the opportunity to make independent editorial decisions based on first-hand knowledge of eighteenth-century performance practices.

Be aware that until the early 1720's French flute music was written in French violin clef (notated a third lower on the staff). It really isn't difficult to read a facsimile edition in French violin clef; simply read bass clef and transpose octaves. Also be aware that in facsimile editions with a basso continuo line, the keyboard part appears as a single figured bass line that has not been realized.

Two retail outlets for facsimile editions are The Early Music Shop of New England (65 Boylston St., Brookline, Massachusetts 02146), and OMI [Old Manuscripts & Incunabula] (PO Box 6019, FDR Station, New York, NY 10150). The following music publishers are known for their facsimile editions:

Autographus Musicus (Bandhagen, Sweden)
Edition Amadeus (Zurich, Switzerland)
Éditions Minkoff (Geneva, Switzerland)
Editions Musicales Aug. Zurfluh (Paris, France)
Frits Knuf (Buren, The Netherlands)
Performers' Facsimiles / Broude Brothers Limited (Williamstown, Massachusetts)
Studio per Edizioni Scelte [abbreviated SPES] (Florence, Italy)

EASY SOLOS

Albinoni, Tomaso (1671–1751)   Italian
Sonata in D Major, no. 5 for flute and basso continuo (c. 1740). Originally published
as *Six Sonatas da camera*
Pub: Amadeus 1974   Edited: Walter Kolneder
Key: D Major (b minor)   Range: d' to e'''
    A very short four-movement work. The Amadeus edition, published as *Due
Sonate,* also includes a sonata in E major.

Bach, Carl Philipp Emanuel (1714–1788)   German
Sonata in G Major for harpsichord and flute (1754) (WOT 85)
Pub: Ricordi (SY634) 1955   Edited: Gustav Scheck, Hugo Ruf
      Breitkopf & Härtel 1955
Key: G Major   Range: d' to e'''
    A charming three-movement work. Easy range, easy rhythms, few accidentals.

Corrette, Michel (1709–1795)   French
Sonata in e minor Op. 25 No. 4 for harpsichord and flute… "Les amusements
d'Apollon chez le Roi Admète"
Pub: Schott 1967   Edited: Hugo Ruf
Key: e minor (E Major)   Range: d' to e'''
    A three-movement work. The Affettuoso second movement is a good way to
begin work in E major, with its range e' to b".

Hotteterre, Jacques (le Romain) (1674–1763)   French
Ecos for solo flute. Published in 1708 in the collection *Pièces pour a flûte traversière.*
Pub: Bärenreiter 1952   Edited: Hans Peter Schmitz
      Schott (ED11631) 1948
Key: G Major   Range: d' to c'''
    A favorite of mine. A brief two-movement work. *Ecos* is found in the back of the
method book *Querflöte und Querflötenspiel* by Hans Peter Schmitz (pub: Bärenreiter).
Available in facsimile edition (French violin clef) from SPES.

Hotteterre, Jacques (le Romain) (1674–1763)   French
Suite in D Major Op. 2 No. 1 for flute and basso continuo. Published in 1715 as
Deuxiéme livre de pièces pour la flûte traversière, et autres instruments, avec la basse.
Pub: Nova Music (NM133) 1979   Edited: David Lasocki
      Musica Rara (2109) 1985   Charles Smith
      Ricordi (SY638) 1955   Gustav Scheck, Hugo Ruf
Key: D Major (b minor)   Range: d' to c'''
    A five-movement suite, easier than Hotteterre's *Suite in e minor.* A good way to
begin the study of French ornamentation which Hotteterre explains in the preface.
The ornamentation makes the suite more difficult than it appears on the surface. Easy
range. Also available in facsimile edition (in French violin clef) from SPES.

Hotteterre, Jacques (le Romain) (1674–1763)   French
Suite in e minor Op. 2 no. 4 for flute and basso continuo. Published in 1715 as
Premier livre de pièces pour la flûte traversière, et autres instruments, avec la basse.
Pub: Nova Music (NM146) 1980   Edited: David Lasocki
      Bärenreiter (3316) 1956   Hugo Ruf
Key: e minor (E Major)   Range: d' to c'''
    A delightful seven-movement suite. Available in facsimile edition (in French violin
clef) from SPES.

La Barre, Michel de (1674–1744)   French
Premier livre de pièces pour la flûte traversiere avec la basse continue. (1702)
Pub: Performers' Facsimiles
Key: D Major, G Major, e minor,   Range: d' to e'''
      g minor, d minor
    A collection of five suites for flute and keyboard. Betty Bang Mather (*French
Noels)* writes that this book is the first edition of pieces written specifically for solo
flute. Begin with the suites in sharp keys; try them first without ornaments. Available
only in facsimile edition (in French violin clef).

La Barre, Michel de (1674–1744)   French
Suite in G Major ("L'inconnue") (1710). Originally published as one of a set of nine
suites in *Deuxième livre de pièces pour la flûte traversiere, avec la basse continuë*
(Paris, 1710)
Pub: Richli 1952
Key: G Major   Range: d' to c'''
    An early work for flute written at the court of Louis XIV. The two movements
(Lentement-Vivement and Chaconne) are written in stepwise motion and contain few
accidentals. Available in facsimile edition (in French violin clef) from Performers'
Facsimiles and SPES.

Loeillet, Jean Baptiste (de Gant) (1680–1730)   Frenchman in England
Sonate in e minor Op. 3 no. 7 (1729). Originally published as *XII Solos, six for a
common flute* [recorder] *and six for a German flute* [transverse flute]
Pub: Leduc 1974   Edited: Pierre Poulteau
      Amadeus 1983
Key: e minor (G Major)   Range: d' to c'''
    An easier five-movement sonata. I played this on one of my first baroque flute
concerts. Amadeus publishes all 12 sonatas in Op. 3 in a four-volume edition (ask for
the volume which contains the e minor sonata).

Marais, Marin (1656–1728) French
Les Folies d'Espagne for solo flute (1701)
Pub: Bärenreiter (BA3311) 1956   Edited: Hans-Peter Schmitz
       Masters Music (M1145) n.d.   Hans-Peter Schmitz
       G. Schirmer (48710) 1987   Louise Moyse
Key: e minor   Range: d' to d'''

   These delightful variations for unaccompanied flute are taken from *Variations in D minor* for viola da gamba. Marais composed them so they could be played on transverse flute as well as on gamba. Graded easy to medium. Also available for flute and basso continuo as published by Leduc (1978) (the Leduc publication keeps the original d minor key) or Zimmerman (1983). Available in facsimile edition (in French violin clef) from SPES.

Marcello, Benedetto (1686–1739) Italian
Sonata no. 12 in G Major. Originally published as *XII Solos for a German flute...Op. l* (1732)
Pub: Editio Musica (Z13476-7) 1989   Edited: István Máriássy
       Amadeus (BP2056-7) 1982   Willy Hess
Key: G Major (e minor)   Range: g' to e'''

   A four-movement work with few accidentals and easy rhythms. Very easy—a good starter piece. All twelve Sonatas are published in facsimile by Performers' Facsimiles and SPES.

Quantz, Johann Joachim (1697–1773) German
6 Sonatas for flute and basso continuo (c. 1730). Originally published by Walsh in London as *Solos for a German Flute, a Hoboy or Violin...Op. 2*
Pub: Müller 1965   Edited: Dieter Sonntag
Key: D Major, G Major, e minor,   Range: d' to d'''
       A Major

   Each sonata consists of four or five short movements. The sonatas are not easy in their entirety, but selected movements make great beginner pieces. Highly recommended.

Quantz, Johann Joachim (1697–1773) German
6 Sonatas for flute and basso continuo. Originally published as *Sei Sonate a Flauto Traversiere Solo, e Cembalo Op. 1.*
Pub: Schott (ED 8007) 1994   Edited: Hugo Ruf
Keys: D Major, e minor, G Major   Range: d' to d'''

   The six sonatas appear in two volumes. I recommend Volume II (sonatas 4, 5, and 6) for its easier keys. Each sonata is a three-movement work.

Quantz, Johann Joachim (1697–1773) German
Sonata in e minor for harpsichord and flute
Pub: Schott (5724) 1968   Edited: Hugo Ruf
Key: e minor   Range: d' to d'''

   A good beginning piece in an easy key.

Ranish, John Frederick (1693–1777)   English
Sonata in b minor, Op. 2 no. 3 for flute and basso continuo (1744). Originally
published as *XII Solos for the German flute...* Op. 2
Pub: Oxford 1971   Edited: Richard Platt
Key: b minor   Range: f' sharp to d'''
    A delightful but easy three-movement sonata with which to begin work in b
minor. Limited range.

Roseingrave, Thomas (1688–1766)   English
Two Sonatas for flute and basso continuo (1728). Originally published as *XII Solos
for a German flute with a Through Bass for the Harpsichord*
Pub: Oxford 1975   Edited: Richard Platt
Key: Sonata #4 in g minor   Range: Sonata #4: d' to d'''
    Sonata #7 in C Major   Sonata #7: e' to c'''
    These four- and five-movement works are short: an entire sonata takes only five to
six minutes. Easy solos for introduction to these less-common keys. All twelve solos
available in facsimile from Performers' Facsimiles.

Telemann, Georg Philipp (1681–1767)   German
12 Fantaisies for flute without bass.
Pub: Amadeus (BP370) 1992   Edited: Peter Reidemeister
    Bärenreiter (2971) 1976   Günter Hauswald
    Musica Rara (2167) n.d.
Key: through 4# and 2b   Range: d' to e'''
    Although these thoughtful, charming works are too difficult for the beginning
flutist, take a look at the final movements of each fantaisie. They are usually dance
movements and somewhat easier than the preceding movements. For unaccompanied
flute. The Musica Rara and Amadeus editions include a facsimile. The Bärenreiter
edition has wrong notes in Fantaisies 11 and 12.

COLLECTIONS

Baroque Flute Pieces 5 volumes
Pub: Associated Board of Royal School of Music 1995   Edited: Richard Jones
Key: Mostly D Major, G Major, e minor   Range: d' to d'''
    A five-volume graded anthology of music of the early and mid eighteenth
century. Volumes I and II recommended for beginners. Volume I consists of twenty-
seven short movements (mostly dance movements). Volume II is a bit more difficult,
and consists of sixteen movements extracted from larger works. Composers include
well-known French, German, and English composers. Beautifully edited. Clear
instruction regarding proper execution of the ornaments. For flute and keyboard with
separate basso continuo part. Highly recommended.

Music for Flute and Basso Continuo 1700–1750
Pub: Oxford 1972   Edited: Richard Platt
Key: various   Range: d' to e'''
    A collection of selected movements from flute sonatas composed 1700–1750. A
good collection representing a variety of styles by English, French, and Italian
composers in various keys.

*The Musick for the Royal Fireworks [and Other Works], set for the German Flute,
Violin, or Harpsichord.*
Pub: Performers' Facsimiles (114) 1993
Key: D Major, G Major, d minor   Range: d' to d'''
    Eleven transcriptions by an anonymous contemporary of Händel. Short, easy
movements (menuets, marches, etc.) drawn from themes in Händel's *Royal Fireworks*
and other works. For one-keyed flute and harpsichord. Available only in facsimile
edition; the keyboard player must realize the figured bass line.

Riley's Flute Melodies (1814 and 1816)
Pub: Da Capo Press 1973   Edited: A facsimile edition
Key: various   Range: d' to g'''
    A collection of nearly 700 short tunes popular in the U.S. during the early
1800's. Most are in D major and G major. Quite easy. Hard cover book. For
unaccompanied flute.

60 Favorite Airs in the Gallant Style
Pub: Fischer 1978   Edited: Betty Bang Mather
Key: various   Range: d' to d'''
    Another favorite collection. Very short, easy pieces for unaccompanied flute.
Includes introduction which concisely and clearly outlines appropriate eighteenth-
century performance practices. At the time of this writing, this collection was out of
print.

30 Virtuosic Selections in the Gallant Style for Unaccompanied Flute
Pub: Fischer 1975   Edited: Betty Bang Mather
Key: various   Range: d' to g'''
    A collection of unaccompanied flute works gathered from six different
eighteenth-century collections. One of my favorite collections. Most works are in one
and two sharps. Range is from easy to difficult. Introduction contains brief, clear notes

A Very Easy Baroque Album, Vol. II
Pub: Novello 1991   Edited: Trevor Wye
Key: various   Range: d' to d'''
    Volume Two consists of eighteen short movements from works by Blavet, Vivaldi,
Philidor, Hotteterre, and Roman. For flute and keyboard. Selections are easy.

Warlike Musick (1760)
Pub: Oxford 1974   Edited: Philip Ledger
Key: D Major, G Major, F Major,   Range: d' to d'''
      e minor
    This edition of 18 short pieces was originally compiled by John Walsh and published in London in 1760. The music reflects the military activity of this period. Published here with basso continuo but some can be performed effectively for unaccompanied flute.
on performance practices.

STUDIES

Frederick the Great and Johann Joachim Quantz   German
Das Flötenbuch Friedrichs des Grossen: 100 Tägliche Übungen für Flöte. [100 Daily Exercises for Flute]
Pub: Breikopf & Härtel (5606) 1934   Edited: Erwin Schwarz-Reiflingen
Key: various   Range: c' to a'''
    These 100 Daily Exercises are extracted from a four-volume set of exercises for flute by Frederick the Great and Quantz. Contains passage work as recommended by Quantz for beginning practice.

Quantz, Johann Joachim (1697–1773)   German
Caprices, Fantasias and Beginner's Pieces for Flute Solo and with Basso Continuo
Pub: Amadeus (BP 2050) 1980   Edited: Winfried Michel and Hermien Teke
Key: through 4# and 7b   Range: d' to a'''
    A collection of sixty etudes and recital pieces. Most range in difficulty from medium to difficult—however, there is a section (beginning with number 24) of short works for flute and basso continuo suitable for the beginner. Some of the music is actually by a fellow named J. M. Blockwitz. The manuscript is located in the Royal Library in Copenhagen.

Quantz, Johann Joachim (1697–1773)   German
Solfeggi pour la flüte traversiere avec l'enséignement, Par Monsr. Quantz (c. 1729–41)
Pub: Amadeus (GM585) 1978   Edited: Winfried Michel and Hermien Teske
Key: through 4# and 4b   Range: d' to g'''
    Even though I would grade this book moderate to difficult, I choose to list it here because every one-keyed flute player should know about it. The studies and excerpts in this notebook formed the basis for Frederick the Great's daily flute practice. It contains Quantz's suggestions for applying inequality and articulation syllables to the musical phrase, as well as alternate fingering suggestions. Facsimile edition by Winterthur (available from OMI). As a companion article, see Claire A. Fontijn, "Quantz's *unegal*: implications for the performance of 18th-century music." *Early Music*, 23:1 (February 1995), 55–62. Quantz's *Solfeggi* is used as a springboard for discussion of *notes inégal*.

EASY DUETS

Blavet, Michel (1700–1768)   French
1e Recueil de Pièces [First Book of Pieces. Little Airs, Brunettes, Menuets, etc]
(ca. 1755)
Pub: Facsimile by Zurfluh 1967
Key: D, G, and F Major   Range: d' to d'''
        e, g, d, and a minor

    Sixty-nine great little unaccompanied duets by Blavet, who used his own themes
and those of other baroque masters. Some tunes have variations or *doubles*. The
beginner might do well to look at the simpler minuets in one and two sharps. Also
available in facsimile edition by Les gravures et impressions musicales A, Brousse—
facsimile is in G-clef. *1e Recueil de Pieces* contains two unaccompanied solos,
including a Gigue which is published in modern edition by Broekmans.

Blavet, Michel (1700–1768)   French
11e Recueil de Pièces (Second Book of Pieces. Little Airs, Brunettes, Menuets, etc)
Pub: Facsimile by Zurfluh 1990
Key: D,'G, and F Major   Range: d' to d'''
        e, g, d, and a minor

    Seventy-three great little unaccompanied duets by Blavet, who uses his own themes
and those of other baroque masters. Some tunes have variations or *doubles*. Again, the
beginner might do well to look at the simpler minuets in one and two sharps.
Facsimile is in G-clef.

Devienne, François (1759–1803)   French
Achtzehn Kleine Flotenduette [18 Little Flute Duets]. Originally published as *Dix huit
Duos* in Devienne's method book called *Nouvelle Méthode* c. 1792.
Pub: Schott 1968
Keys: Through 3# and 2b   Range: d' to e'''

    Devienne, one of the first professors of flute at the Paris Conservatory, composed
music in the classical style for the one-keyed flute. These duets are very easy and
contain few ornaments. I highly recommend you read them with a friend; you'll learn
a great deal about intonation by playing easy duets. Available in facsimile by
purchasing Devienne's method book *Nouvelle Méthode* (pub: SPES).

Devienne, François (1759–1803)   French
Six Duets for two flutes Op. 82
Pub: Peters (Nr. 8366) 1973   Edited: H. Bohme
        International (1655) n.d.
        Belwin 1976
Key: D Major, G Major   Range: d' to f''' sharp

    These duets are quite easy; they contain very little ornamentation. Each of the six
duets has two movements.

Fesch, Willem de (1687–1761)   Dutch
Six Sonatas for two flutes Op. 9 (1743)
Pub: Universal (UE19512) 1995   Edited: Gerhard Braun
Keys: D Major, G Major, a minor,   Range: d' to e'''
        d minor, e minor
   This Dutch composer lived the last thirty years of his life in London and wrote in
the style of Händel. Some of these sonatas are challenging, so begin with the easier
movements in the easier keys. Well-written and carefully edited.

The French Noel   French
Pub: Indiana Univ. Press 1996   Edited: Betty Bang Mather & Gail Gavin
Key: D Major, d minor   Range: d' to d'''
   In 1725, an anthology of French Noels was published for flute duet. These short
and easy duets are republished here, complete with scholarly chapters on noel forms,
dance steps for early noel melodies, and performance of noel melodies. Recommend
"for those wishing to learn the true art of playing the little French airs." See Chapter
Four "Performance of Noel Melodies" for tips on performance practices.

Händel, Georg Friedrich (?) (1759–1803)   German
Six Sonatas for two unaccompanied flutes. Originally published in Paris by LeClerc.
Pub: Zanibon (6325) 1994   Edited: Gian-Luca Petrucci
Key: e minor, G Major, A Major,   Range: d' to e'''
        b minor, D Major, E Major
   We are not certain that these fine duets can be attributed to Händel. However, they
display originality and I highly recommend them. Each sonata has four movements.
They are not easy, but lie well under the fingers.

Bibliography Before 1853

Alexander, James. *Alexander's Improved Preceptor for the Flute*. London: J. Sandford, c. 1830.

> Tunes from this instruction book for amateur flutists are used in this method book.

Arnold, [Samuel]. *Dr. Arnold's New Instructions for the German-Flute*. London: Harrison & Co., 1787.

> Tunes from this instruction book for amateur flutists are used in this method book.

Bach, Carl Philipp Emanuel. *Versuch über die wahre Art das Clavier zu spielen*. Berlin: the author, 1753. English translation by William J. Mitchell published as *Essay on the True Art of Playing Keyboard Instruments* (New York: W. W. Norton, 1949; London: Cassell, 1951).

> Contains helpful information on ornamentation and rhythmic hierarchy.

Blavet, Michel. *le Recueil de Pieces: Petits, Airs, Brunettes, Menuets, etc.* Paris: by the author, c. 1755. Facsimile reprint, Paris: Editions Aug. Zurfluh. n.d.

> Tunes from this book for amateur flutists are used in this method book.

Cahusac, Thomas. *Cahusac's Pocket Companion for the German Flute*. London: Printed and sold by T. Cahusac, c. 1780.

> A copy of this little book is housed in the rare book room at the Rita Benton Music Library at the University of Iowa. Tunes from this instruction book are used in this method book.

Corrette, Michel. *Méthode pour apprendre aisément à jouer de la flûte traversière*. Paris: Boivin & Le Clerc, c. 1734. English translation by Carol Reglin Farrar published by the Institute of Mediaeval Music as *Michel Corrette and Flute-Playing in the Eighteenth Century* (Brooklyn, New York, 1970).

> One of the "Top 13" eighteenth-century flute tutors. See Appendix A.

Couperin, François. *L'Art de toucher le Clavecin*. Paris: the author, 1716. English translation by Margery Halford published as *Couperin: L'art de toucher le clavecin* (Port Washington, New York: Alfred Publishing Co., 1974).

> Contains useful information on ornamentation. With introductory notes.

The Delightful Pocket Companion for the German Flute. London: R. Bremner, c. 1763. A reissue of the edition published by J. Simpson in c. 1745.

> Tunes from this instruction book for amateur flutists are used in this method book.

Delusse, [Charles]. *L'art de la flûte traversière*. Paris: the author, c. 1760. Facsimiles published by Éditions Minkoff (Geneva, 1973) and Frits Knuf (Buren, The Netherlands, 1980).

> One of the "Top 13" eighteenth-century flute tutors. See Appendix A.

Devienne, François. *Nouvelle méthode théorique et pratique pour la flûte*. Paris: Imbault, c. 1792. Facsimile edition published by Studio per Edizioni Scelte (Florence, Italy, 1984). Modern English translation in William Montgomery's Ph.D. dissertation "The Life and Works of François Devienne, 1759–1803" (Catholic University, 1975).

> One of the "Top 13" eighteenth-century flute tutors. See Appendix A.

Fürstenau, Anton Bernhard. *Die Kunst des Flötenspiels.* Leipzig: Breitkopf & Härtel, 1844. Facsimile edition published by Frits Knuf (Buren, The Netherlands, 1990). English translation by Janet E. Houston in her D.M.A. dissertation *The Art of Flute Playing by A. B. Fürstenau: Translation and Commentary* (The Juilliard School, 1994).

> A. B. Fürstenau played a keyed flute. In his treatise, he declares that the one-keyed flute is definitely a German invention, supplied by the Nuernberg flute-maker Denner.

Geminiani, Francesco. *Rules for Playing in a True Taste on the Violin, German Flute, Violoncello, and Harpsichord.* London: by the author, c. 1747.

> Geminiani's brief two-page introduction to eighteen pages of music gives the reader insights into what he considered "good taste."

——————. *A Treatise of Good Taste in the Art of Musick.* London, 1749. Facsimile edition published by Da Capo Press (New York, 1969). Introduction by Robert Donington.

> A good general eighteenth-century performance practice reference. Contains four charming airs with an Irish flavor for flute and figured bass.

Granom, Lewis. *Plain and Easy Instructions for Playing on the German-Flute.* Third Edition with Additions. London: T. Bennett, c. 1770.

> One of the "Top 13" eighteenth-century flute tutors. See Appendix A.

Gunn, John. *The Art of Playing the German-Flute on New Principles.* London: the author, c. 1793. Facsimile edition published by Janice Dockendorff Boland (Marion, Iowa, 1992). With introduction by Janice Dockendorff Boland.

> One of the "Top 13" eighteenth-century flute tutors. See Appendix A.

Hawkins, Sir John. *A General History of the Science and Practice of Music.* First publication in 5 vols., London: Payne and Son, 1776. Reprint, 2 vols., New York: Dover, 1963.

Heron, Luke. *A Treatise on the German Flute.* London: W. Griffin, 1771.

> One of the "Top 13" eighteenth-century flute tutors. See Appendix A.

Hotteterre, Jacques. *Principes de la flûte traversière, ou flûte d'Allemagne. . .* Paris: Christophe Ballard, 1707. English translation with introduction by David Lasocki published by Praeger as *Principles of the Flute, Recorder and Oboe* (New York, 1968).

> One of the "Top 13" eighteenth-century flute tutors. See Appendix A.

James, William Nelson. *A Word or Two on the Flute.* Edinburgh: Charles Smith & Co., 1826. Third edition, with additional introduction. London: Tony Bingham, 1982.

> A charming little nineteenth-century book which speaks frankly of the early flute players and performance considerations.

Keith, Robert William. *A New & Complete Preceptor for the German Flute.* London: the author, c. 1815.

> See Keith's account of flute embouchure and tone production.

Lindsay, Thomas. *The Elements of Flute-Playing.* London: the author, 1828–30.

> A substantial English flute tutor. Contains information regarding flute care and repair, and beating time. Exercises from Lindsay's tutor are used in this method book.

Longman and Lukey. *Longman and Lukey's Art, (in Miniature) of blowing or playing on ye German Flute.* 2 vols., London: the authors, c. 1775.

> Tunes from this instruction book for amateur flutists are used in this method book.

Lorenzoni, Antonio. *Saggio per ben sonare il flautotraverso.* Vicenza: Francesco Modena, 1779. Facsimile edition published by Forni (Bologna, Italy, n.d.) with introduction in Italian by F. Alberto Gallo.

> One of the "Top 13" eighteenth-century flute tutors. See Appendix A.

Mahaut, Antoine. *Nieuwe Manier om binnen korten tyd op de Dwarsfluit te leeren speelen./ Nouvelle Méthode pour apprendre en peu de tems à joüer de la flûte traversière.* Second edition. Amsterdam: J. J. Hummel, 1759. English translation by Eileen Hadidian published by Indiana University Press as *A New Method for Learning to Play the Transverse Flute* (Bloomington, Indiana, 1989).

> One of the "Top 13" eighteenth-century flute tutors. See Appendix A.

Mattheson, Johann. *Das Neu-Eröffnete Orchestre.* Hamburg: Benjamin Schillers, 1713.

> A good source for reading about the passions assigned to particular keys in early eighteenth-century music. Partial English translation by Rita Katherine Steblin in her Ph.D. dissertation "Key Characteristics in the 18th and Early 19th Centuries: A Historical Approach" (University of Illinois, 1981).

—————. *Der volkommene Capellmeister,* 1739. English translation by Ernest C. Harriss published by UMI Research Press (Ann Arbor, MI, 1981).

> A good source for the study of rhythmic hierarchy (English translation pages 344–63).

Miller, Edward. *The New Flute Instructor.* London: Broderip & Wilkinson, c. 1799.

> An English instruction book for amateur flutists.

Mozart, Leopold. *Versuch einer gründlichen Violinschule.* Augsburg: Johann Jacob Lotter, 1756. English translation by Editha Knocker pub. by Oxford University Press as *A Treatise on the Fundamental Principles of Violin Playing* (London, 1948, 1951, 1985).

> The father of Wolfgang Amadeus Mozart writes about ornamentation and violin bowings, which give us insight into articulation practices and rhythmic hierarchy.

Muffat, Georg. Preface to *Florilegium Secundum.* Passau, 1698. Ed. H. Rietsch, *Denkmäler der Tonkunst in Österreich,* Jahrgang 2/2 (Vienna, 1895). Transl. by Kenneth Cooper and Julius Zsako, "Georg Muffat's Observations on the Lully Style of Performance." *Musical Quarterly* 53 (1967), 220–245.

> Selected references regarding meter and performance are cited by George Houle in an article published in *Historical Performance*. See Houle entry in this bibliography.

Müller, August Eberhard. *Elementarbuch für Flötenspieler.* Leipzig: Peters, c. 1815. Modern English translation in Margaret Stevens Lichtmann's D.M.A. dissertation "A Translation with Commentary of August Eberhardt Müller's *Elementarbuch für Flötenspieler*" (Boston University, 1982).

> Müller was a highly respected German composer and performer. His tutor is for both the one-keyed and the flute with additional keys and contains 45 pages of exercises.

Nicholson, Charles. *School for the Flute.* London: 1836. Facsimile edition
published by Peter H. Bloom (Somerville, MA., n.d.).
> This nineteenth-century flute tutor gives instruction on how to beat time (pp. 16–17).

Playford, John. *A Breefe Introduction to the Skill of Musick for Song and Violl.*
London, 1654. Facsimile edition of the 12th ed. (London, 1694) published
by Zimmerman (New York, 1972).
> This seventeenth-century tutor gives instruction on how to beat time.

[Prelleur, Peter.] *The Modern Musick-Master or the Universal Musician.* London:
Printing-Office in Bow Church-Yard, 1730. Facsimile edition by Bärenreiter
(London, 1965). Edited by Alexander H. King.
> One of the "Top 13" eighteenth-century flute tutors. See Appendix A.

Quantz, Johann Joachim. *Versuch einer Anweisung die Flöte traversiere zu spielen.*
Berlin: Johann Friedrich Voss, 1752. English translation by Edward R. Reilly
published by Schirmer Books as *On Playing the Flute* (2nd edition, New
York, 1985).
> One of the "Top 13" eighteenth-century flute tutors. See Appendix A.

Rousseau, Jean. *Méthode Claire.* Paris: 1678.
> This seventeenth-century source explains how to beat time (p. 31).

Saint-Lambert, Michel de. *Les Principes du Clavecin.* Paris: 1702. English
translation in part by Carol MacClintock, *Readings in the History of Music in
Performance* (Bloomington: Indiana University Press, 1979).
> Source for articulation silences. See MacClintock pp. 222–223.

Simpson, Christopher. *Compendium of Music.* London: 1665.
> This seventeenth-century source explains how to beat time.

Tomlinson, Kellom. *The Art of Dancing.* London: the author, 1735. Facsimile
edition by Gregg International Publishers Limited (Brookfield, VT, 1970).
> This eighteenth-century dance tutor explains how to beat time. Includes descriptions of
many dances, complete with dance notation and music.

Tromlitz, Johann George. *Ausführlicher und gründlicher Unterricht die Flöte zu
spielen.* Leipzig: Adam Friedrich Böhme, 1791. English translation by
Ardal Powell published by Cambridge University Press as *The Virtuoso Flute-
Player* (Cambridge & New York, 1991).
> One of the "Top 13" eighteenth-century flute tutors. See Appendix A.

Tulou, Jean-Louis. *Méthode de Flûte.* Mainz: Schott, 1853. Modern English
translation by Janice Dockendorff Boland and Martha F. Cannon published as
Jean-Louis Tulou, A Method for the Flute (Bloomington: Indiana University
Press, 1995).
> A French instruction book, included here because its tunes and exercises are used in
this method book. Although Tulou is known for his work with keyed flutes, he shows
a fingering-chart for the one-keyed flute.

Türk, Daniel Gottlob. *Klavierschule...* Leipzig and Halle, 1789. English translation
by Raymond H. Haggh, University of Nebraska Press as *School of Clavier
Playing* (Lincoln, Nebraska, 1982).
> Part Four (pages 88–104) provides the reader with helpful information on rhythmic
hierarchy and meter.

Vanderhagen, Amand. *Méthode nouvelle et raisonnée pour la flûte.* Paris: Boyer, c. 1790.

> One of the "Top 13" eighteenth-century flute tutors. See Appendix A.

_____. *Nouvelle méthode de flûte.* Paris: Pleyel, c. 1800. Facsimile edition by Studio per Edizioni Scelte (Florence, Italy, 1984).

> Contains information on beating time. Tunes from this instruction book are used in this method book.

Vaucanson, Jacques de. *Le mécanisme du fluteur automate = An account of the mechanism of an automaton; or, Image playing on the German-flute.* Paris: Jacques Guerin, 1738. English translation by J. T. Desaguliers (London: T. Parker, 1742). Facsimile edition of both English and French texts by Frits Knuf (Buren, The Netherlands, 1979).

> An account of a mechanical flute. Important for its discussion of embouchure and tone production.

Wragg, J. *The Flute Preceptor; Or The Whole Art of Playing the German Flute.* London: the author, c. 1792.

> An English instruction book for amateur flutists. Tunes from Wragg's tutor are used in this method book.

BIBLIOGRAPHY AFTER 1853

Babitz, Sol. *The Great Baroque Hoax. A Guide to Baroque Performance for Musicians and Connoisseurs.* Los Angeles: Early Music Laboratory, 1970.
> Strongly opinionated but helpful, particularly as a reference on rhythm.

Barlow, Jeremy. *The Music of John Gay's The Beggar's Opera.* Oxford & New York: Oxford University Press, 1990.
> A good source of information about the tunes and text from the Beggar's Opera.

Bloom, Peter H. *A Practical & Tuneful Method for the Baroque Flute.* Somerville, Massachusetts: Peter H. Bloom, 1989.
> First modern tutor for the baroque flute. Especially helpful for the student with no modern flute background. Easy solos and duets.

Bowers, Jane. "The French Flute School from 1700 to 1760." Unpublished Ph.D. dissertation, University of California, Berkeley, 1971.
> Includes a discussion of the tutors by Hotteterre, Corrette, and Delusse.

Bowers, Jane. "New Light on the Development of the Transverse Flute between about 1650 and about 1770." *Journal of the American Musical Instrument Society*, III, 1977, 5–55.
> Lots of helpful illustrations included.

Cameron, Roderick. *Please Read These Instructions Before Assembling and Playing Your New Flute.* Mendocino, California: Cameron, 1988.
> Instructions for flute care that accompany the purchase of a Cameron flute.

Carse, Adam. *Musical Wind Instruments, a History of the Instruments used in European Orchestras and Wind Bands from the Later Middle Ages up to the Present Time.* London: 1939. Reprint, New York: Da Capo Press, 1965.

Cramer & Co's. Improved Flute Preceptor. London: Cramer & Co., c. 1880.
> Tunes from this instruction book for amateur flutists are used in this method book.

Cyr, Mary. *Performing Baroque Music.* Portland, Oregon: Amadeus Press, 1992.
> Highly recommended reading. Accessible and informative.

Dannreuther, Edward. *Musical Ornamentation.* London and New York: Novello, 1893–1894. Reprint, New York: Kalmus, 1961.

Dart, Thurston. *The Interpretation of Music.* New York: Harper & Row, 1963.
> A general introduction to such topics as musical style, ornamentation, and sonorities.

Dolmetsch, Arnold. *The Interpretation of the Music of the XVII and XVIII Centuries.* London: Novello, 1915. Second edition, 1946. Reprint, Seattle: University of Washington Press, 1969.
> An important early twentieth-century study of performance practices.

Donington, Robert. *Baroque Music: Style and Performance.* London: Faber Music, 1982; New York: Norton, 1982.

_____. *The Interpretation of Early Music.* London: Faber and Faber, 1974; Rev. ed. New York: Norton, 1989, 1992.
> See especially pages 414–416 for information on beating time.

_____. *A Performer's Guide to Baroque Music.* London: Faber and Faber, 1973; New York: Charles Scribner's Sons, 1973.
> Robert Donington's helpful books are standards in the field of early music.

Fontijn, Claire A. "Quantz's *unegal*: implications for the performance of 18th-century music." *Early Music,* 23: 1 (February 1995), 55–62.
> An especially good article on rhythmic inequality or *notes inégales.* Fontijn uses Quantz's *Solfeggi* as a springboard for discussion.

Gärtner, Jochen. *Das Vibrato.* Regensburg: Gustav Bosse, 1974. English translation by Einar W. Anderson published as *The Vibrato, with Particular Consideration given to the Situation of the Flutist* (Regensburg: Gustav Bosse, 1981).
> Gartner surveys the history of the use of vibrato on the flute.

Giannini, Tula. "Jacques Hotteterre le Romain and his father, Martin." *Early Music,* 21: 3 (August 1993), 377–395.
> Giannini takes a new look at the Hotteterre family of flute-players and flute-makers.

Hartman, Donald H. "Pedagogical Practices Relating to the German Flute in England from 1729 to 1847." Unpublished D.M.A. essay, Eastman School of Music, Rochester, New York, 1961.
> Hartman discusses in detail the contents of the more important English flute tutors dating 1729–1847.

Haynes, Bruce. "Beyond temperament: non-keyboard intonation in the 17th and 18th centuries." *Early Music,* 19: 3 (August 1991), 357–381.
> An especially good article on tunings for wind instruments. Haynes includes eighteenth-century flute tutors in his references.

—————. "Generic 415." *Traverso,* 1: 4 (October 1989), 1–2.
> Haynes challenges the twentieth-century pitch standard for the one-keyed flute by asking why we should accept A-415 as the standard.

—————. "Tu ru or Not Tu ru…." *Performance Practice Review,* (Spring 1997), 41–60.
> Haynes looks at tonguing syllables for transverse flute as found in tutors dating 1700–1827.

Helm, Ernest Eugene. *Music at the Court of Frederick the Great.* Norman, Oklahoma: University of Oklahoma Press, 1960.
> Helm takes us inside the Court of Frederick the Great for a look at the musical scene, complete with Quantz, C. P. E. Bach, and others. One of my favorite books.

Houle, George. "Meter and Performance in the Seventeenth and Eighteenth Centuries." *Historical Performance,* 2: 1 (Spring 1989), 11–19.
> Good source for study of rhythmic hierarchy and meter.

—————. *Meter in Music 1600–1800: Notation, Perception, and Performance.* Bloomington: Indiana University Press, 1987.
> An in-depth look at rhythmic hierarchy, "good" notes and "bad" notes.

Jones, William John. "The Literature of the Transverse Flute in the Seventeenth and Eighteenth Centuries." Unpublished Ph.D. dissertation, Northwestern University, Evanston, Illinois, 1952.

Krueger, Christopher. "Playing Baroque Music on the Modern Flute." *Flutist Quarterly,* 13: 1 (Winter 1988), 44–53.
> Krueger addresses issues of historically informed performance, touching on vibrato, ornamentation, and tonguing for players of both modern and historical flutes.

Lasocki, David. "The Baroque Flute and its role today." *Recorder and Music Magazine,* 2: 4 (February 1967), 99–100, 104.

_____, editor. *Fluting and Dancing. Articles and Reminiscences for Betty Bang Mather on her 65th Birthday.* New York: McGinnis & Marx, 1992.
> Betty Bang Mather is a foremost authority on one-keyed flute playing and associated performance practices. This Festschrift in her honor contains several articles relating to those subjects and others.

Lawrence, Eleanor. "Interview with Shelley Gruskin." *The National Flute Association, Inc. Newsletter*, 4: 3 (Spring 1981), 3, 10–13, 18.
> Shelley Gruskin is one the first twentieth-century wind players to play the one-keyed flute professionally. The interview is very insightful.

LeRoy, René. *Traité de la Flûte; historique, technique, et pédagogique.* With the collaboration of Claude Dorgeuille. Paris: Editions Musicales Tansatlantiques, 1966. English translation by Marcia Fatout published as *Treatise on the flute, historical, technical, and pedagogical by René LeRoy.* (Available from University of Iowa Rita Benton Music Library.)

MacClintock, Carol. *Readings in the History of Music in Performance.* Bloomington & London: Indiana University Press, 1979.
> A collection of texts and translations from historical sources from late Middle Ages to the early nineteenth century.

McGowen, Richard Allen. "Italian Baroque Solo Sonatas for the Recorder and the Flute." Unpublished Ph.D. dissertation, University of Michigan, Ann Arbor, Michigan, 1974.

Mather, Betty Bang. *Interpretation of French Music from 1675 to 1775 for Woodwind and Other Performers.* New York: McGinnis & Marx, 1973.
> Mather covers such relevant topics as articulation practices, rhythmic inequality, and ornamentation as recommended by eighteenth-century flutists Hotteterre, Corrette, Delusse, Quantz, Mahaut, Devienne, and Vanderhagen.

_____. *60 Favorite Airs in the Gallant Style.* New York: Carl Fischer, 1978.
> Contains an easy-to-undertand introduction filled with performance instruction.

Mather, Betty Bang, and Gail Gavin. *The French Noel. With an Anthology of 1725 Arranged for Flute Duet.* Bloomington: Indiana University Press, 1996.
> Noel melodies are published here in the form of simple flute duets. Chapter Four is devoted to performance practice and shows the flutist how to play these noels and similar French pieces from this period.

Mather, Betty Bang, and David Lasocki. *The Art of Preluding 1700–1830 for Flutists, Oboists, Clarinettists and Other Performers.* New York: McGinnis & Marx, 1984.

_____. *The Classical Woodwind Cadenza: A Workbook.* New York: McGinnis & Marx, 1978.

_____. *Free Ornamentation in Woodwind Music 1700–1775.* New York: McGinnis & Marx, 1976.
> I highly recommend Mather and Lasocki's publications. They contain abundant musical examples and direct language which lead the one-keyed flutist (and other players) painlessly through performance practice considerations.

Mather, Betty Bang, with Dean M. Karns. *Dance Rhythms of the French Baroque.* Bloomington: Indiana University Press, 1987.

Miller, Dayton C. *Catalogue of Books and Literary Material Relating to the Flute and Other Musical Instruments.* Cleveland: the author, 1935.
> An annotated catalogue of books, magazine articles, pamphlets, and newspaper clippings from Miller's private collection.

Neuhaus, Margaret. *The Baroque Flute Fingering Book.* Naperville, Illinois: Flute Studio Press, 1986.
> A comprehensive guide to fingerings for the one-keyed flute, including trills, *flattements,* and *battements.*

Neumann, Frederick. *Ornamentation and Improvisation in Mozart.* Princeton, New Jersey: Princeton University Press, 1986.

_____. *Ornamentation in Baroque and Post-Baroque Music.* Princeton, New Jersey: Princeton University Press, 1978.
> A somewhat controversial tome (over 600 pages) dealing with ornamentation. Lots of musical examples.

_____. *Performance Practices of the Seventeenth and Eighteenth Centuries.* New York: Schirmer Books, 1993.
> See *Part I: Tempo* for information on rhythmic hierarchy. *Part VI: Ornamentation* is divided by country (France, England, Germany, Italy) so the reader can determine how the performance of ornaments varied from one musical center to another.

North, Roger. *Roger North on Music: Being a Selection from His Essays Written during the Years c. 1695–1728.* Edited by John Wilson. London: 1959.

Poor, Mary Louise. "Problems of Transference from Boehm to Baroque Flute." *The National Flute Association Inc. Newsletter,* 6: 3 (Spring 1981), 6–7.
> The observations of a teacher who teaches beginners the one-keyed flute.

Powell, Ardal. "Baroque Flute Maintenance." *Pan,* 8: 1 (March 1990), 30–31.
> A good article on the care of the one-keyed flute.

_____. "The Hotteterre Flute: Six Replicas in Search of a Myth." *Journal of the American Musicological Society,* 49 (Summer 1996), 225–263.

Reilly, Edward Randolph. *Quantz and His Versuch.* American Musicological Society, Studies and Documents, No. 5, 1971. (Distributed by Galaxy Music Corrporation, New York).

Rockstro, Richard Shepherd. *A Treatise on the Construction, the History, and the Practice of the Flute.* London: Rudall, Carte, 1890. Revised edition, 1928. Reprint by Frits Knuf (Buren, The Netherlands, 1987).
> Covers history of the development of the flute, the art of flute-playing, and biographical and critical notices of sixty eminent flute-players.

Smith, Catherine Parsons. "Characteristics of Transverse Flute Performance in Selected Flute Methods from the Early 18th Century to 1828." Unpublished D.M.A. thesis, Stanford University, Stanford, California, 1969.
> Written by a player of historical flutes drawing from historical sources and personal experience.

Solum, John, with Anne Smith. *The Early Flute.* Oxford: Clarendon Press, 1992.
> Advice regarding purchase and care of the one-keyed flute, lists of respected makers, and an abundance of references make this a helpful book for today's one-keyed flutist.

Toff, Nancy. *The Development of the Modern Flute.* New York: Taplinger
    Publishing Co., 1979; Urbana: University of Illinois Press, 1986.

_____. *The Flute Book.* Second Edition. New York: Oxford University
    Press, 1996.

>   *The Development...* gives the reader a history lesson in flute-making and *The Flute
>   Book* contains profiles of prominent flutists and flute repertory.

Vester, Frans. *Flute Music of the 18th Century.* Monteux, France: Musica Rara,
    1985.

>   An exhaustive catalogue of eighteenth-century solo and chamber music for flute.

Warner, Thomas E. *An Annotated Bibliography of Woodwind Instruction
    Books, 1600–1830.* Detroit: Information Coordinators, Inc., 1967.

>   The reference bible for locating flute tutors dating 1600–1830.

_____. "Indications of Performance Practice in Woodwind Instruction Books
    of the 17th and 18th Centuries." Unpublished Ph.D. dissertation, New York:
    New York University, 1964.

Waterhouse, William. *The New Langwill Index: A Dictionary of Musical Wind-
    Instrument Makers & Inventors.* London: Tony Bingham, 1993.

>   A reference work which includes lists of flute-makers, their marks, the location of their
>   shops, and the dates they worked.